PARADISE
IN FRONT OF ME

PARADISE
IN FRONT OF ME

Realizing Life's Beauty in an Unexpected Place

Kevin G. Finch

A PEACE CORPS WRITERS BOOK

A Peace Corps Writers Book
An Imprint of Peace Corps Writers Worldwide

First Peace Corps Writers Edition, January 2014

Paradise in Front of Me. Copyright © 2014
by Kevin G. Finch

Library of Congress Control Number: 2013944327
ISBN-13: 978-1-935925-24-8
ISBN-10: 1935925245

Book Design by Matt Musselman

Printed in the United States of America

A PEACE CORPS WRITERS BOOK

For my wife, Cristina

Acknowledgements

The venture of writing this book began with a few simple emails. I would like to thank my friends, mostly the alumni of Broad Run High School and James Madison University, who took the time to read my messages, believed I had a good story to tell, and encouraged me to write this book.

Roanoke, Virginia is full of talented people who are willing to share their expertise and time with others. I give special thanks to Sue Ross, Jim Morrison, Jane Henderson, and Vince Mier for working tirelessly to proofread and edit this manuscript. Matt Musselman, a friend and neighbor, took time out of his busy life to design the cover for this book. Without the skills, encouragement, and support of each of these individuals, this book would be likely still just a dream of mine.

I am privileged to live in a country where one is afforded the opportunity to serve abroad. I thank the Peace Corps and everyone who was part of the Honduras team for providing me the life-changing opportunity to live and work in El Paraíso.

My love of writing truly began in high school. At that time, I was not a fan of things like sentence structure and grammar. Fortunately, I had wonderful teachers along the way who not only encouraged me to write but inspired me to do it well. A special thanks to Ruth Keiper and Norma Bornarth, two of the best writing teachers to ever grace the hallways of Broad Run High School, who never settled for mediocrity in my writing.

It was not until college that I discovered that you learn most about yourself and life when you are open to serving others. I thank Fr. John Grace for not only teaching me this valuable lesson but for being a living example of it.

While I was working on this book, I was fortunate to meet Betty Price. I thank her for reminding me of the power of the written word and for inspiring me with her gargantuan love of language.

In my early years as a writer, I was impatient, overconfident, and not very open to criticism. Somehow, one person put up with all of this and still took time to help me out. I thank my mom, Barbara Finch, for staying up late with me so many nights to fine-tune my writing, for encouraging me to do my best, and, most importantly, for believing in my ability to write something others would want to read.

When times were tough in Honduras, there was always someone there to pick me up. Nobody was more a source of encouragement and support than my dad, Dennis Finch. He replied to every email I ever sent, and his positive responses were always just what I needed to hear. Thanks, Pops.

A lot has changed since I began writing this book. Most notably, I have been blessed with two new additions to my family. To my beautiful daughters, Adelaide and Bridgette, thank you for postponing reading a story or playing a game so that Dad could finish this book.

I thank my wonderful wife Cristina. For thirteen years, we have been experiencing the adventures of life together. Thank you for always believing in me, for encouraging me to finish this book, and for choosing me to be your partner on this beautiful life journey.

Finally, this book would not exist without the wonderful people of El Paraíso, Honduras. Words cannot do justice to the impact they have had on my life. Thank you for so willingly opening your lives to two strangers and for teaching me what makes life so special.

Author's Note

In September 2012, citing concerns for the safety and security of the volunteers, the Peace Corps suspended activities in Honduras and withdrew its volunteers.

The New Student

November 12, 2009

It's 8:30 a.m., and I'm ready to go home. "Come on everyone, let's get where we need to go. You're all going to be tardy," I say to a group of students cluttering up the hallway. A teenage girl rolls her eyes at me and another makes an effort to move slower. *This is pointless.* Most of my students have arrived, so I turn to gain control of my tiny corner of this large middle school in Southwest Virginia. I glance at the stack of papers on my desk, try not to think about the mounting to-do list, and remind myself of the three parents I need to call. *At least it's Friday.*

Before I can close the door, there's a tap on my shoulder. *What now?* I spin around trying fruitlessly to hide my aggravation. "Here he is." Becky, the English Language Learner teacher, has her hand around the shoulder of a short, stocky young boy. He looks terrified. "This is Orlin, the child from Honduras. It's his first day, and he doesn't speak any English," she says smiling at him. "I wanted you two to meet."

The chaos around me fades into the background as I shake Orlin's hand. In him, I see a small part of my story. In his smile, I see *their* optimism. In his eyes, I see *their* struggle. "Come in," I say in Spanish. "It's nice to meet you."

My class quiets down. Orlin sits in the front row staring up at me. I drop my head. *How quickly I forget.* "Okay, everyone, let's get started." Papers shuffle and the chatting subsides. I take a step back and gaze around the room at the group of young children that are such

i

a large part of my life. A big smile stretches across my face. *Yes, there it is: paradise in front of me.*

Prologue

I will never forget the first moment I laid eyes on Honduras. Leaning across my wife, Cristina, and looking down from the airplane, I saw the beautiful blue water splashing softly along the coast. Up to that moment, Honduras had been nothing more to me than a small color on a big map. From the plane, I was looking at what would be my home for the next two years.

My story is not really about the country of Honduras. It is about a place in Honduras, a small town nestled in the southern mountains only a few miles from Nicaragua.

El Paraíso (Paradise) is, as I've heard other places described, a land of contradictions. Beautiful, lush green mountains being devastated by deforestation; a center of town with rows of cute one-story homes and businesses sitting on dusty roads littered in garbage; kind, humble people living in poverty so extreme your heart breaks on a daily basis.

This book is an attempt to capture the essence of living in a small town in a Third World country. The stories you will read and the people you will meet are real and were part of the life my wife and I led for two years between 2004 and 2006 when we served as Peace Corps Volunteers. I never planned to write a book about this experience.

Paradise in Front of Me began as nothing more than monthly emails to my family and close friends. The subject heading was always "Hello from Honduras." To my surprise, these simple emails began to touch lives. As the two years progressed, the number of people reading my emails had jumped to over 100, and the feedback I got from the stories was humbling. People were intrigued with life in El Paraíso, wanted to hear more, and eventually began sharing their own perspectives on life there as I described it. The support of our friends and family, and their sincere interest in our experiences, helped us make it through some difficult times and also inspired the writing of this book.

The book encompasses the observations of two Americans who come from backgrounds different in so many ways from those in El Paraíso. By sharing a little about the people, the culture, and our work, I hope to provide a fair and accurate view of life in El Paraíso.

This book is honest. In these stories, my wife and I share our daily frustrations which at times may seem harsh and overly critical. Looking back, I would agree some of them are. To leave these observations out would not be fair, even if the words and thoughts seem offensive. These descriptions of life capture how we truly felt in the moment. The book is not always a feel-good book, but El Paraíso is rarely a feel-good place. It is, however, a place that taught us more about life than any place ever will. For this, we will always be grateful for our two years there. I hope you enjoy the journey.

PARADISE
IN FRONT OF ME

Reality Check

February 2, 2004

I wake up well before the alarm goes off and look over at Cristina sleeping peacefully. I am jealous because my mind is racing. Last night I watched the New England Patriots beat the Carolina Panthers in the Super Bowl and Janet Jackson's wardrobe malfunction. I was surrounded by my family, new-born nephew, and my best friend of 25 years. Now, 12 hours later, I am about to leave all of this and my very comfortable life in the U.S.A. Suddenly, I have trouble breathing.

It is a brisk, cold morning in Washington, D.C., as my father-in-law drives us to Reagan National Airport. As we pass the monuments representative of our great country, I attempt to imagine the place I am about to go. I cannot.

My mother, father and sister meet us at the airport to say farewell. We enjoy breakfast, and I cherish every minute of the time with my family. I am filled with so many emotions: sadness, excitement, and fear, just to mention a few. Finally the time comes to say our good-byes. It will be a year before we see our families, and my mom and sister are crying. We all hug several times, and I, like a good son, assure my mom that we will be fine. I promise to tell her whenever I need anything.

As we make our way through the post 9-11 security clearance line, Mom takes out her camera for a photo. She wipes her tears and snaps a picture. She looks ready to take another when a rather large security guard motions to two larger security guards. They begin

1

moving rapidly towards my mother who is apparently violating a security code. And, so I fear, the last memory of my mother, before leaving home for the longest period of my life, will be of her being tackled by two security officers. Fortunately, Dad sees what is happening and motions to Mom. She puts away her camera and waves. As Mom disappears out of sight, I squeeze my wife's hand and think, *What are we about to do?*

How did we get to this point? I find it flattering that so many people wanted to know what made us decide to join the Peace Corps. Only my mother wasn't surprised. She knew, as she said the day I informed her of our intentions, that this was something I had to do or would regret forever.

Over a year ago, even before we got married, Cristina and I discussed our futures. We were both ready for a life change but not yet ready to settle down and start a family. I was 29, Cristina 25, and we both felt we were beginning new chapters in our lives. We wanted to live in another country, experience a different culture, learn a second language, and challenge ourselves in new ways. The Peace Corps was the obvious answer.

I've noticed something interesting in my life, a sort of pattern. I--in this case we--develop an idea for a new adventure. I plan it out, share it with my family and friends and get very excited. The excitement lasts up until about a month or two before I'm set to begin. Then I get scared, wonder if I jumped into something without considering all of the consequences, and want to bail out. I don't want to leave my family, my friends, and the comfortable life I'm living, even though I know it's time to move on. I once read that "God comforts the uncomfortable and discomforts the comfortable." I've felt that in my life. The reality of joining the Peace Corps was no exception.

The fear that I made the wrong decision usually continues well into my time in the new environment. Honestly, I don't really appreciate the risk taken and the positive impact it had on my life until well after I've moved on to something else. So, I am in a sort of daze as I hold the hand of my new bride and walk toward our gate. I don't know what to expect, nor do I want to imagine. The adventure is about to begin, and there is no turning back. "The toughest job you'll ever love." We are about to find out.

Welcome to Honduras

We leave Washington, D.C., and land in Miami, Florida, for a brief two-day introduction to the Peace Corps. This is where we have one last chance to say, "No thanks!" It is surreal to say the least.

After a whirlwind of an introduction, we awake at the crack of dawn in our very nice hotel room in Miami. I have to pry Cristina's fingers from the fluffy pillows and remind her, as I certainly will again and again, that this was her idea too. We scurry around the room, gathering our belongings and shoving them into four suitcases that will somehow sustain us for two years. Then it is off to the airport with 60 other strangers where we board a plane and make haste for Central America.

If the plane ride and subsequent landing are any indication of what the next two years will be like, I am now considering asking the pilot to turn around. Seated next to me on the plane is a friendly fellow Peace Corps Volunteer who I instantly judge "Least Likely to Last a Month." She pours her heart out to me at 40,000 feet. It seems she already doubts her decision. There is a boyfriend back home, and she doesn't think they can make the long distance thing work. How would he stay faithful for so long? Could she blame him if he didn't? Was she risking too much by following her desire to be a Peace Corps Volunteer? Should she have more faith and leave this in God's hands? Having just spent five minutes pondering whether to order the orange juice or a soda, I am in no position to handle these questions. I feign active listening while wondering, *What is her name? Is it too late to pretend*

4

to be asleep? Should I have ordered a bourbon? When she concludes her story, I say, "Just take things one day at a time." She likes that idea and thanks me for listening. Miss "Least Likely to Last a Month" ends up lasting 27 months and being one dang good Peace Corps Volunteer. Just call me Dr. Phil.

As we approach Toncontín Airport in Tegucigalpa, Honduras (try saying that with a mouthful of airline peanuts), we begin our descent. Perhaps a better way to say "descent" would be "Hang on for your $%!* life!" For about 10 seconds, I'm certain we're all going to die. The plane dives quickly, turns at a 90-degree angle, and points one wing to the ground with the other straight up in the air. I pray, peek out the window at the people on the ground who are ducking, and pray again.

The guy across the aisle from me, whom I judge "Peace Corps Volunteer Least Likely to Last One Week," is bear hugging the seat in front of him and mumbling something that sounds like, "Mommy." I grip the armrests with everything I have while Cristina digs her fingernails into my forearm. I don't feel a thing. I am too busy trying not to wet myself. The pilot flattens out the plane, drops it down immediately onto a runway disguised as a driveway and slams on the brakes.

When the plane finally stops, one can hear a pin drop. After a collective, "What the heck was that?" we erupt in applause. I exhale and then smile. It is as if Honduras is saying, "Hey, Kevin, you'd better get ready for one wild ride."

Marriage

Cristina and I were married in June, and we laughingly refer to Peace Corps as our honeymoon. Some people mentioned that the Peace Corps might not be the best way to start a marriage. After all, adjusting to married life can be a difficult task; why tack on the additional stress of leaving family, moving to an unfamiliar place, and everything else that can make life as a Peace Corps Volunteer challenging. Were they right? Were we making a mistake?

We met on the dance floor. It was a brilliant May afternoon in Atlanta, Georgia. A friend of mine and I were sitting on the bleachers of a high school gym. We had decided to give swing dance classes a try. They were offered through a singles group, and we figured it might be a fun way to meet some people as we were both new to the city. Basketball and baseball were my life growing up, so this was my first dance class. I still wasn't sure what I was doing there. Then, she walked into the gym. I remember her long, dark brown hair hanging just below her shoulders as she moved across the floor. She was beautiful.

The instructor lined the boys up on one side of the gym and the girls on the other. Immediately, I was taken back to middle school. I got nervous. Most in the group of 40 people were in their 30s and 40s which made me feel better. I was 26 and was content learning some swing dance moves and hanging out with good people. The prospect of meeting my future wife never crossed my mind.

"Okay everyone," the instructor shouted as she stood in between the two lines, "Now, move across the floor and partner with the person directly across from you." The two lines moved forward, and at that moment I realized *she* was walking directly towards me. We met in the middle of the floor. Her brown eyes looked up at mine, and I was smitten.

We dated for three years before marrying in 2003. At no point did I ever doubt my love for her. She is confident in who she is, and she doesn't sacrifice her morals or beliefs for anyone. She is passionate about her work, always looking for ways to improve things to make life easier for others. I never doubted her love for me. For the first five months of 2002, Cristina left Atlanta to study abroad in Australia. "Aren't you worried?" my friends asked. The truth is I wasn't. We talked weekly, emailed daily, and the time flew. I arrived in Sydney in June 2002 to spend the summer with her. After exiting the plane, I saw her moving towards me through the terminal. My heart started beating rapidly. I reached frantically into my hip pouch to make sure it was still there. It was. I felt the round shape of the ring just before she flew into my arms.

Cristina and I have always been a great team. I couldn't imagine doing something like Peace Corps without her. I wasn't worried about our marriage, but I also didn't know what to expect.

Our Assignments

Although Cristina and I are serving together in Peace Corps, we are a part of two different projects. Upon arriving at our training site, we will begin three months of intensive language and project training.

Cristina has advanced degrees in city planning and civil engineering. As a result, she has been assigned to work in the Municipal Development Program. Projects within this program are designed to help municipal governments improve their ability to deliver public services while empowering youth and other citizens to actively participate in local government. This is a vague description of a program with many specific goals and objectives. Her work will be based largely on the needs of the community where we are placed.

I spent the past four years working in the Georgia public school system as a special education teacher and recently completed my master's degree. I've been assigned to the HIV/AIDS and Child Survival Program. The focus, however, will be on education. Health education resources are lacking in Honduras. My duties will include working with community health workers and other leaders in order to assess and monitor the health of the community. I will target children and women of reproductive age and provide them with nutrition information and strategies for preventing common and deadly illnesses (e.g., diarrhea, malnutrition). Another focus of the program is training and empowering youth leaders to provide education on HIV/AIDS to adolescents in the community. According to the Peace Corps, HIV/AIDS is a growing health problem in Honduras and incident rates continue to increase. Again, my exact roles and responsibilities will depend on the needs of the community.

We are both excited about our assigned projects and itching to get started.

Immersion or Thrown to the Wolves

We exit the plane, gather our belongings, and jump onto a school bus that takes us to Santa Lucia, the place we'll call home for the next three months. After a few hours of introductions and a crash course in survival Spanish, it is time to meet our host families. Before diving into a description of the lovely family with whom we will live, let me explain the extent of my Spanish skills. I took two evening courses at a local college in Georgia. After the approximately 40 hours of coursework, I was able to count to ten and ask for the location of a bathroom. One of these two skills would prove vital.

On this beautiful crisp evening in Santa Lucia, Cristina and I are introduced to María and Luis. When it comes to being paired with a host family, we have hit the Peace Corps jackpot. María and Luis live in a lovely little home with an indoor bathroom and a shower head equipped with an *electraducha*. An *electraducha* is a contraption that hooks to the shower head and heats the water as it comes out. It's an absolute luxury in Honduras to shower with hot water. Heck, it's a luxury just to have a shower.

María and Luis are a young couple who share a wonderful trait: they have smiles that can light up a room. Those smiles are priceless as I struggle daily with the reality that I cannot communicate with them effectively. I feel frustrated and useless sitting at the kitchen table while Cristina, who picks up the language rapidly, laughs and talks with María and Luis while I pretend to understand. I just don't feel like myself when I can't communicate. Fortunately, our hosts are wonderful teachers who show enormous patience and encourage me daily to keep trying.

Luis has worked hard to create a good life for his family by Honduran standards. He is a bus driver who runs daily trips from Santa Lucia to another town about 45 minutes away. He drives the same route every day from about 7 a.m. to 8 p.m. Every morning, he gets up before daylight, grabs some breakfast, and starts up his bus which sits parked in the front yard. He is smiling from the moment he wakes up to the moment he drags his tired body in the front door after dark each night. His only day off is Sunday, when he spends a good part of the day sleeping. He never complains, only occasionally hinting he wishes the work days weren't quite so long. When he gets home, he wants only to hear about our day. After a long, difficult day maneuvering the crazy streets of Honduras, Luis refuses to be served his dinner until Cristina and I are seated, served, and ready to eat.

While Luis and María do not have any children of their own, they have taken in three children from a mother who is in the United States. Many more kids float in and out of the house during our time here as well. I feel most comfortable around the children. They don't care what I'm like, where I'm from, or what language I do and do not speak. If I'm willing to play with them, I'm one of them. We play soccer every day, a wonderful diversion from the homesickness and frustration I feel during training. I can't imagine these first few months without the kids and their unwarranted kindness and beautiful laughter.

Training

Training has been an exhausting experience. The day begins with a morning briefing. We are given the schedule for the day, updates on any volunteers who may have decided to call it quits (there have been three so far), and reminders that our behavior does reflect upon the Peace Corps and our country. This is directed at the group members who find alcohol the best way to deal with being a volunteer.

Mornings are often spent in Spanish classes. We are grouped by ability and classes are extremely small, 3-4 students. The teachers are Hondurans. They are amazing. They make the monumental task of learning a new language enjoyable, despite all of the frustration I am feeling. While my language skills have improved considerably, I still feel woefully unprepared to be effective as a volunteer. My teachers continue to tell me that I will be fine. I want to believe them. My speaking skills are adequate, but I have tremendous difficulty understanding when someone speaks. My goal is to try to capture one word or verb in a sentence that may help me unravel the message being communicated. It is a laborious task, and I wonder if I will ever grasp the language.

After language classes, it is time for lunch. Lunches are prepared by the host families, and once again Cristina and I are reminded that María and Luis are the best. It is comical to watch each volunteer open his Tupperware container to reveal the inner contents. A crowd usually gathers around Cristina and me as we open ours, the anticipation growing. "Oh, that's not fair!" someone inevitably shouts. "That looks delicious!" Crowds gather around other volunteers for the opposite reason. We can't resist the temptation to see what weird concoctions have been created by other host families. "What is that?" "Is that even edible?" Suddenly, I am back in elementary school, watching classmates barter in an attempt to land a better food option. Fortunately, Cristina and I have no need to do this.

The unusual meals created by some host families are confusing, because generally Honduran food is pretty simple. Rice and beans are the staple of the Honduran diet, especially in the more impoverished areas. The *baleada* is a favorite. It is a tortilla filled with beans; sometimes eggs, cheese, avocado, and meat are added. The *plato típico* is a popular dinner. It is meat, beans, cheese, and avocado. I love the *plato típico*. María and Luis generally eat *baleadas* or *plato típico* for dinner. Lunch is usually *baleadas* or pasta with green beans and cheese. Eggs are also common. In the more impoverished areas of Honduras, the families live off of corn tortillas, beans, rice, and eggs. Pasta can be purchased at local *pulperías* (small convenience stores), and some families do eat pasta occasionally. There is a variety of local and seasonal fruits and vegetables that are consumed in addition to these staples.

Now it's time for the afternoon sessions. Usually the afternoon is dedicated to training in specific project areas. My classes focus on nutrition, especially for mothers and children, and HIV/AIDS prevention. The lessons are a combination of cultural and medical training. Our mission is not only to share the information we are learning, but most importantly, also to train local adults and youth to do our job. I am bombarded with an extraordinary amount of information, but the extent to which I will use this new knowledge will depend largely on the town or village to which I am assigned.

The Bus to Linaca

As my language skills gradually improve, I quickly learn that there is a lot more to communication in a foreign land than the language. I find this out the hard way in a town called Danlí during the second month of training.

A fellow volunteer and I have been assigned to make an information gathering trip to a small community named Linaca. Our instructor informs us that a bus leaves for the town at 12:20 p.m. and another at 2:30 p.m. One other bus returns from Linaca at 5 p.m. We decide we need to catch the 12:20 bus if we want to have enough time to get our work done and return.

At noon, we arrive at the location where we believe the bus will depart. Sure enough, there is a bus that says "Linaca." The hood of the bus is up and a young man is working on the engine. "Does the bus to Linaca leave at 12:20 p.m.?" I ask. "Yes it does," he replies. "Okay, we're early, so we'll be back by 12:20," I say. "Okay," he responds with a big smile.

We get something cold to drink and return at about 12:15. The hood of the bus is still up, and the same man is now inside the bus trying to get it started. A couple of other people, though not many, are standing around waiting. As we watch patiently from the sidewalk, the man starts the bus. He pulls forward, with the hood still up, and plows into a parked pick-up truck a few yards in front. With a big smile, he looks at us and shrugs his shoulders as if to say "oops." I am already dreading the ride we are about to take.

At 12:25, I decide to ask the driver when we will be leaving. "At 2:30," he states, without hesitation. "What? What happened to 12:20?" I yelp. "Oh," he says, wiping his hands with a greasy rag. "That bus already left." I am sure I have heard wrong. We arrived at 12:00 and, when we returned at 12:15, the same man and the same bus were in the exact same place. "The 12:20 bus already left?" I ask, hoping for a different response this time. He is busy working on the engine, doesn't look up, and replies, "Yes, it left from the other street five minutes ago." *The other street? Where was the other street?* "This is not where the bus to Linaca leaves from?" I ask in desperation. "No, it leaves one block up," he says with his head down and arm pointing to the right.

I want to throw something. This man never said a word as we stood waiting for the bus for 15 minutes. He is a nice gentleman and doesn't seem to find anything strange about our conversation. As far as he is concerned, he said nothing that wasn't true. Yes, there was a 12:20 bus to Linaca and it left, as he said, at 12:20. We never asked where the bus left from, and he never told us.

As I've come to discover, the situation was totally my fault. Many people do not offer additional information. They rarely elaborate and will answer a direct question with a direct answer only. It's my job to ask all the questions necessary to get a thorough response. I should have asked, and I'm not being sarcastic, "Is this bus, this bus right here, going to leave for Linaca from this location at 12:20 p.m.?" He likely would have said, "No," and nothing else. I would then ask a series of questions to reach the correct conclusion about the bus to Linaca.

I'm learning that communication is completely different here, in a manner that goes far beyond language, and I'm learning the hard way. I have spent a lot of time angry at my seeming inability to gather information correctly. Now I'm beginning to accept it as a fundamental cultural difference and realizing it is my job to figure it out.

AIDS

It's the end of March, and I've been in Honduras for almost two months. Between adjusting to living in Honduras and trying to learn Spanish, I'm just plain tired. I miss Cristina. Training lasts three months, two of which are spent in Santa Lucia. However, one month is spent in another city depending on the assigned program. Since Cristina and I are in different programs, we are spending this second month on opposite ends of the country. Needless to say, I am ready to be finished with this phase of the Peace Corps process. However, this morning I'm in for a jolt.

We all take our seats in a circle, as we do every morning, and are briefed about the events of the day. I yawn and try to look interested. We are told we will have a guest speaker named Emilia. A young, attractive Honduran woman enters the room and takes a seat in the circle. My supervisor explains that today, after weeks of reading and studying, we will have the opportunity to experience the reality of Acquired Immune Deficiency Syndrome (AIDS) in Honduras. I perk up. *Surely this woman does not have AIDS.* She does and will share her story with us for the first time. I'm on the edge of my seat. At age 18, Emilia met her eventual husband, Ernesto. They dated and got married. After six years of marriage and the birth of two children, Emilia began to fear Ernesto was sleeping around. Ernesto assured her that he wasn't, but she was still fearful. She asked him to be tested for HIV. He did and told Emilia he tested negative. He lied. A year later, Emilia tested positive for HIV. Fortunately, her children are healthy. Emilia speaks for an hour, weeping softly most of the time. This is the first time she has told her story out loud, and I imagine hearing it this way must be heartbreaking. She's reliving the nightmare.

There is not a dry eye in the room by the time she finishes her story. Emotions are mixed when Emilia leaves to confront her future. We now have a face to our mission, and it has reenergized us.

In our group, we discuss something else that made Emilia's story so heart wrenching. She did not do drugs. She did not sleep around. Emilia fell in love with a man, got married, and remained faithful to him. In other words, she followed a path that we as Peace Corps volunteers will emphasize in our work with the youth and adults of this country. Emilia, however, never had a chance.

Reflections on Training

Back in Santa Lucia, Cristina and I are relieved as the final week of training approaches. We've been consumed in this training bubble for three months now and it has been a difficult and draining experience. We are in Honduras, but it doesn't feel like we are really in Honduras. We are surrounded by Americans, living with a host family that is living comfortably compared to many, and in a picturesque little town. Training has been an effective, well-run process. We've been impressed with everyone involved--Hondurans and Americans alike. Our fellow volunteers are an unbelievable mix of ages, personalities, and backgrounds. Some will be great volunteers, I am certain. Cristina and I, while still anxious about the next step, are ready to move on from training.

The Big Day

Perhaps the most exciting moment of our service in the Peace Corps has arrived. It's the day we receive our site assignments. For three months, Cristina and I and our fellow volunteers have tried unsuccessfully to determine where we will be living for the next two years. Don't we each have that itch to pull out a map, close our eyes, point to a spot, and go?

I'm handed a folder and slowly peek inside. The paper says, "El Paraíso" which translates to "Paradise." *Oh baby*! A small dot in the Southeast corner of Honduras marks the location of our new home. After a celebration with our fellow volunteers, Cristina and I race home, excited that we are finally ready to embark on this great adventure. We grab the *Moon Handbook Guide to Honduras* and flip to "El Paraíso." Surely paradise is awaiting us. Page 173 reads, "El Paraíso does not offer much beyond its proximity to the Nicaraguan border. Should you *need* (emphasis added) to spend a night in this town . . ." Hmm, that sounds, well, uninspiring. We don't care. We have spent over a year working to get accepted into the Peace Corps and another three months enduring difficult training. We're ready to go. Paradise, here come the Finches!

El Paraíso

Cristina and I awake to the sunlight beaming through a transparent section of corrugated plastic in the roof otherwise referred to as our skylight. I rub my eyes and try to orient myself. We don't need an alarm clock here. At 4:00 a.m., the first rooster breaks the early morning silence, and by 5:00 several more have joined in. At 5:30, our neighbor starts his car and prepares to leave for his farm. By 6:00, El Paraíso is alive and moving. It's time to begin our day.

I can't roll out of bed, like I normally would. First, our bed takes up most of the room; second, the entrance and exit to our bed is at the foot. Hanging from the ceiling and covering the entire bed is a mosquito net. The blood-thirsty insects are more than just a nuisance here in Honduras as they carry debilitating and deadly illnesses. While not as well known as Malaria, Dengue Fever is a prevalent viral disease carried by mosquitoes that makes one extremely sick. In cases involving the most vulnerable, primarily the very young and very old, it can kill. So, while the net surrounding our sleeping quarters is irritating at times, we do not complain.

I slide out of the net and look around the house we now call home. It is the size of a small one-bedroom apartment in the U.S. but compared to many in Honduras, it is large. My first stop is at the *pila*. The large basin is about three feet tall and six feet wide. It is our water source, and this morning it is about a third of the way full. I scoop some cold water out with a small green bucket and wash my face. With one hand, I grab a towel hanging from our indoor clothesline and with the other turn on the faucet. We make sure the *pila* is full first thing in the morning.

We have luxuries in our house that most in the surrounding, more rural areas, do not. We have an indoor *pila*, indoor plumbing, and running water from about 5 a.m. to 10 a.m. most days. We never know for certain when the water will be turned on or off, so when it's available, we fill the *pila*. We will soon find out that there will be days when the water never flows. The *pila* is the lifeline of our home. We use the water to take a bath, wash our clothes, boil for cooking, flush the toilet (by pouring water from a bucket into the toilet to force everything down the drain), wash the dishes, brush our teeth, etc. An empty *pila* makes for a miserable day.

It's a bit chilly this morning, so the idea of a morning bath is not appealing. One of our first purchases in El Paraíso was a giant blue bucket. When it's bath time, I use the small green bucket to transfer water from the *pila* to the blue bucket that sits in our shower. It's a shower only in the sense that it has a drain and a shower curtain. A "bucket bath" involves using the green bucket to scoop water from the blue bucket and then pouring the water over one's body. A "bucket bath" takes about 30 seconds because it is not a pleasant way to bathe. Again, I cannot complain. This entire process takes place indoors. In the rural countryside, *pilas* are usually filled with water carried from a well. Baths are taken outside. This morning, I forgo the bath and move to the kitchen.

I grab a cup off the shelf and fill it with water from a five gallon bottle of purified water that sits upside down on a small dispenser. Access to the purified water, a mini fridge that rests under our counter, and a two-burner electric stovetop we use for all of our cooking are all items left by previous volunteers that many in and around our town cannot afford.

As I contemplate breakfast, I hear commotion behind our house and slip out the screen door onto our porch. The porch is only about 150 square feet with a six-foot-high cinderblock wall separating us from our neighbors. Doña Romany is our landlord; she and her extended family occupy the house attached to ours on the right as well as two others that, when connected with our neighbor on the left, form a square around an open area that serves as a private driveway and outdoor gathering space. This morning, there is a bunch of bananas resting on the top of our wall, a gift from Doña Romany. Breakfast is served.

The neighbor to our left is unique, and one that I do not recommend. In fact, if one enjoys quiet as well as the ability to sit on the porch without fear of getting struck by an errant soccer ball, it's just about the worst neighbor one could want. This neighbor, with whom we share a wall, is an elementary school. Recess might as well be in our living room.

I gobble down two bananas while Cristina monitors the *pila* which is now almost full. It's time to run some errands, so I step out the front door onto the street. El Paraíso is dirty. Trash is strewn throughout the streets. Dogs run freely, and their crap must be avoided by those on foot. A pickup truck comes racing around the corner, kicking up clouds of dust. It's miserable living a few feet off of a dirt road that also happens to be a major thoroughfare connecting El Paraíso to the distant villages speckled throughout the mountains around us. Dust from the streets gets into everything, irritates our noses and eyes, affects our breathing, and carries a variety of health problems. Residents of El Paraíso sweep and mop their floors several times a day in an effort to keep things clean. I curse the dust. As soon as I've mopped, it is back covering the floor. Cristina conveniently has a "dust allergy" I wish I had claimed first.

The pickup truck zips past me, filled with people from the mountains coming to town to either work or shop. The faces of the people in the cab of the truck are expressionless and covered in dust. Most have a shirt or towel over their mouths as they endure the extremely long and uncomfortable journey.

First on my list is a trip to the *pulpería* to pick up some bread, eggs, and milk. These tiny convenience stores, most the size of a large bedroom, are located on each block and sell just about everything one needs to survive in El Paraíso. Because the *pulperías* are so prevalent and sell the same products, it's no wonder that very few make much money. In addition, many of the items sold in the stores can also be purchased from street vendors throughout the city. Speaking of street vendors, it's time for me to head to the town square to stock up on a few other items.

The square is buzzing this morning. Taxi cabs are lined up on one end, waiting to take travelers to nearby towns. I avoid the cabs at all costs. Most are very old cars that are literally falling apart. It's a tribute to Hondurans that they are able to keep these vehicles running. Cab drivers in this town make U.S. drivers seem safe, so I travel on foot wherever possible. This morning, people are walking back and forth throughout the square, carrying plastic bags full of various items. I receive a mix of odd looks and friendly greetings. I approach a street vendor, spit out a few words in Spanish, and hope for a tomato, carrot, green pepper, and onion. The vendor obliges, although I have to repeat *zanahoria* (carrot) several times before finally pointing to it. He smiles and nods, as if to say, "Oh, that's what you meant." Blessed with fertile soil and a climate that does not vary greatly, fruits and vegetables are plentiful and widely available here. Across the street is a bank where I go to handle all issues involving our finances. Guarding the front door is a short, skinny man holding an enormous rifle. He smiles and nods as I enter, and I smile and nod bigger. I do not want to upset him. Throughout El Paraíso, in front of every bank and large store, are heavily armed guards. Their presence is meant to send a very clear and not-so-subtle message: Don't even think about trying to steal something. Message received, thank you very much.

I head for home, admiring the tall green mountains that separate Honduras from Nicaragua. It begins to drizzle, and I'm grateful for the rain that will pack down the dirt road and give some reprieve from the dust. As I turn down our street, I immediately need to bob and weave to avoid the stream of Honduran children, clad in their blue and white uniforms, who are heading towards the school. My "neighbors" are arriving.

Carlos

Having grasped the basics of our new lifestyle, we are itching to get down to business. As a municipal development volunteer, Cristina plans to spend most of her time offering assistance to local government employees, community development leaders, the Chamber of Commerce, the *Casa de la Cultura* (Cultural Center), and the Tourism Commission. The list is an impressive one, but the extent of her work with these groups will vary greatly. Her counterpart, the Honduran she is assigned to work with, is Carlos, a man with too many responsibilities and not enough time.

Carlos' brain never stops running. He thinks big, dreams big, and is one of El Paraíso's most precious resources. He loves art, music, and the natural beauty of the El Paraíso countryside. He is the owner of a special café in town, *Café D'Palo*, where he and other members of his family can be found playing live music and singing every Saturday night.

Carlos is a visionary living in a box. I wonder how he stays so positive. He is in charge of the local *Casa de la Cultura*, owner of his café, director of the volunteer tourism commission, band teacher at a local elementary school, husband, and father of four children. He is the hardest working person in El Paraíso, and he doesn't have much help.

Carlos has too many ideas. Some nights when we drop by the café for a drink, he bounces around behind the bar, letting us in on his latest vision for El Paraíso. He serves us our drinks and paints his picture of the town as a booming tourist destination with a rich art and music scene that is the envy of Honduras. It sounds wonderful, and we nod and smile along with him, a Renaissance man living in the wrong place. We want to feel his excitement, share his vision, but we just can't. We've been here a short time but long enough to know that most of this will not get done in his lifetime, if ever. We wonder if Carlos knows this as well, as if sharing his dreams is a way to make living in El Paraíso more bearable. Maybe the grand vision of what El Paraíso could be helps keep his mind off of what it is. It gives him hope.

The Statistics

I have been assigned to assist the Health Center in their campaign to prevent the spread of HIV/AIDS. My counterpart is Erika, a dedicated nurse. She works, like all of the employees at the Health Center, in very difficult conditions. Less than 15 nurses and one doctor are assigned to maintaining the health of nearly 40,000 people.

The statistics on HIV/AIDS in Honduras are alarming to say the least. Upon our arrival, Honduras had 24,000 reported cases of HIV/AIDS. The United Nations (UN) estimated this number to be closer to 60,000 or more, due to the fact that many cases go unreported. Honduras has 20 percent of the Central American population yet 60 percent of the HIV/AIDS cases.

The majority of these cases are along the San Pedro Sula corridor, stretching along the north coast of Honduras, far from the quiet town of El Paraíso. There seems to be a false sense of security here, a feeling that the deadly hand of AIDS won't stretch this far. But a few cases have popped up, and when you learn about the sexual practices of young people in El Paraíso, you know you are sitting on a time bomb. Fortunately, Erika knows this better than anyone I've met.

The Tree

It's a spectacular morning in El Paraíso. The sun is shining brightly, the sky is a cloudless blue, and the mountains appear even closer than usual. I close the door behind me, wave to the neighbors, utter something that may or may not be Spanish, and head to the Health Center. A building the size of a mid-size, one-level house in the U.S., the Health Center is overcrowded, understaffed, and a downright disaster area. However, there is good news: The Health Center is expanding.

Standing in the way of this expansion is a large coconut tree. The government of El Paraíso has dispatched a trio of young men to send the tree to the forest in the sky. The three men, armed with a bicycle (their mode of transportation) and an axe (their tool of preference) are on the scene and ready to go. In El Paraíso, apparently, an event like the cutting of a tree is big news. As I enter the front door of the Health Center, I notice most people are heading out the back door. I see Janet, a nurse I met a week ago, and join her to view the event. The tree cutters, after a few seconds of looking around, seem to have concurred on this plan of attack: Whack the tree and hope for the best.

Judging from the way the three men are encircling the tree, the following possibilities are in play: 1) the tree falls directly forward and either falls just short of or utterly demolishes a small wooden structure where a man sells snacks; 2) the tree falls to the right, crashing over a short concrete wall, into some power lines and possibly on top of a house on the other side of the street; or 3) the tree falls left and

27

seriously damages the Health Center which in this moment is hoping to expand, not collapse. Grab your popcorn folks, 'cause this is going to be good.

With a mighty swing of the axe, the gala begins. The crowd is muttering. I, on the other hand, am growing increasingly worried. I honestly cannot believe what is taking place. I try telling Janet that the tree cutters may be about to cause a huge disaster. She is half paying attention as the crowd of about 30 or 40 people is growing more excited with each swing of the axe. I plead my case to no avail. It's as if everyone is saying, "Sure, there is probably a better way to do this, but isn't this way more interesting?" As the tree begins swaying, I realize that we are probably endangering our lives by standing so close to the action. I work my way slowly back through the crowd, hoping that the tree falls safely. Whack, whack, whack. . . .

A final swing of the axe is followed by a deafening moment of silence. The tree leans and sways. It creaks and crunches. And then it falls . . . *right*. The great beast crashes over the concrete wall, falls into the electrical lines, bends the electric poles, and comes to rest in the middle of the road, just a few feet from the house across the street. I stare in utter disbelief.

The silence lasts several seconds and is followed by what can only be described as a collective "*Dios Mío!*" (Oh my God!) From amid the commotion, the owner of the nearly destroyed home comes flying out of his front door, clad only in a pair of red boxers and waving his arms like a wild man. I have no idea what he is saying, but he looks ridiculous, and I have to laugh. And then I can't stop laughing, as I stare at the aftermath. The poor tree cutters are standing in a circle around the stump scratching their heads and no doubt hoping for a do-over. The homeowner in his boxers keeps yelling at the tree like it has just decided to lie down and take a nap in his front yard. The crowd begins to disperse, but I don't move. I am new to El Paraíso, and I sense that what I have just witnessed is much more than a random crazy incident. The entire event seems to reveal something about the culture in which I am now living. My deep contemplation is interrupted by the sound of an approaching bicycle. The electric company is arriving on the scene, and what a scene it is!

A Mess

The last few weeks have been very frustrating for Cristina and me. Honduras is going through a difficult time right now. Things seem a bit crazier than even people here are accustomed. For the past two to three weeks, there has been a nation-wide teacher strike. The kids have been out of school during this time, and the entire country is suffering. The teachers block the main highways between the capital, Tegucigalpa, and the industrial center, San Pedro Sula, located several hours to the north. A good part of the Honduran economy is dependent on travel between these two cities. The president is forced to do something which inevitably angers another group of people and results in another strike. I've heard the arguments from both sides, and after much thought and drinking, have arrived at this conclusion: Things are a mess!

The last thing this country needs is its children out of school. I've traveled all around El Paraíso, from schools in the center of the city to one-room school houses in the mountains. In the city center, schools are adequate buildings with large classrooms. Due to a lack of space, half of the student body attends school from 7 a.m. to 12 p.m. and the other half from 12 p.m. to 5 p.m. The rooms are filled with old wooden desks and chairs.

Each teacher has approximately 40 students in each class. Discipline is impossible. There is an enormous lack of resources. Many teachers guard their chalk like it is gold. The children do not have textbooks, so they must copy down information from the teacher or from an old book. Students rarely if ever participate in class. If you enter a classroom for the first time and ask kids for their input, they'll stare at you, waiting for the right answer. I once witnessed two high school students doing homework at the local library. I asked them about it. They told me that their homework was to copy five pages out of a book, word for word. I asked them why and they replied, "We have no idea." I can't get over how normal it is to see kids copying like that out of a book. Otherwise, they spend a lot of time coloring. From the sounds of the school next to our house, recess makes up about half of the school day. I don't know how anyone is learning anything.

Walking into a classroom in the mountains is like stepping into a time machine. There is one teacher in one room with up to 40 kids ages six to 14. There are few resources and trying to determine what the kids are doing is nearly impossible. It's very sad. The teachers try, but in five hours with kids of all ages, how can they accomplish anything? There is only one high school in El Paraíso, serving kids from miles and miles away. Many children live in the distant mountains where there is no transportation, and attending the school is unrealistic. There are two students in a distant mountain village who awaken at 5:30 a.m. to make the 1 ½ hour bike ride to the school. At least going is downhill.

Most families don't have enough money to purchase a notebook, much less a bicycle. If a child's family can't afford a uniform, the child is not permitted to attend school! There are children in El Paraíso who are sitting at home doing nothing because the uniform is too expensive. It is for reasons like this that almost half of the students in Honduras never complete primary school (6th grade). Considering that nearly half of the 6.5 million people in Honduras are under the age of 15, this is a very scary fact.

So, watching this strike take place makes one feel helpless. I have a friend, Humberto, who stands at the corner of our street every day selling chips and candy out of a tiny wagon he has made out of wood. He works daily from about 7:30 a.m. to 5:00 p.m. I estimate that his family lives off of two or three U.S. dollars a day, about average for many in El Paraíso. He has a child and desperately wants her life to be better than his. He's furious, to put it nicely. He recently said to me, "How can a country develop like this? How can a country ever develop without education?" Pointing to his daughter, a look of utter frustration on his normally smiling face, he says, "How will things ever be better for her?"

It's Not Fair

Each year, for a few months, the nurses from the Health Center head out to the most remote parts of El Paraíso. They go door-to-door ensuring that all children under five years old have received proper vaccinations. Without this campaign, children would certainly die. Erika, my soft-spoken counterpart, thinks that this is an excellent way for me to learn more about the surrounding areas.

Erika is a fascinating woman who says little and rarely reveals any emotion. She is overworked and underpaid. She works in nearly impossible conditions, does so with very limited resources, and attacks her job with a passion that is admirable. She doesn't offer me much information but will answer any question I have with honesty.

Today, I follow her as we travel on foot from house to house in the mountains of El Paraíso. We come to one home which, like the others, is a combination of wood and packed dirt, with a tin roof and dirt floors. I stand outside for just a moment, admiring the spectacular countryside around me. Then I duck my head and enter. The sight I witness is one that I will never forget.

Seated in a plastic chair, covered in a thin white net, is a young girl of about 12 years. Her head, also covered by the white net, is tilted back in an awkward position. Her wrists and hands, poking out from beneath some old, musty towels, are horribly contorted. Her knees are bent up close to her body and beneath the towels I can see two terribly disfigured feet. She cannot weigh more than 80 pounds. She cannot speak and saliva falls slowly from the corner of her mouth. The odor of the towels covering her body makes me gag. Occasionally the white net slips from her face, and she is swarmed by flies that have all but taken over the house. The flies crawl in her mouth and eyes, and she winces slightly. A family member quickly runs to swoosh away the flies and replace the net.

It is her large, beautiful eyes that are so striking to me amid this heartbreaking scene. Whenever a family member mentions her name, the young girl smiles, and her eyes light up. Then the smile leaves her face and her eyes close slightly. Her mother explains that they cannot afford to take her to Tegucigalpa, which is three hours away by bus, to see a doctor, much less pay for any medical bills. There is nothing they can do but love her, which they are obviously doing.

Erika can read my thoughts and gives me a comforting smile as she turns and walks out the door of the house. This is her reality. My admiration for her continues to grow. I grab the pack of supplies and fall in line behind her as we scurry down a narrow path to our next destination.

The image will stay with me forever. No one should have to live like this young girl. What does she think about every day? Is she happy or is every day torturous? I have no way of knowing. My struggles and challenges here are small, as are those of many people by comparison. Her life is a reminder of that, and I am mad at myself for needing her struggle to teach me such a lesson. I leave her humble home shaken and thinking that what I have just witnessed is simply not fair.

The Tourist Perspective

The strikes have been going on now for over a month. I head to the newsstand in the park to pick up a paper and keep up with what's taking place. It has been a dismal month for those here and throughout the country. Our work has been halted, and we are anxious for things to return to normal. As I leaf through the pages, I come across a quote from a U.S. tourist who happened to be in Tegucigalpa during the strikes. Her response opened my eyes to how careful I must be when making observations about life in a new place. She said how proud she was of the Honduran people. It was wonderful to witness the nonviolent protests and see the Honduran people sticking up for what they believe in. She would, she said, go back to the U.S. to share this wonderful experience with her friends.

What an injustice to all of the people, especially the children, who are suffering as a result of a very unstable and difficult time. If she spent any time at all here, she would understand that these strikes accomplish nothing and cripple much. Strikes are so common that nobody takes them seriously. She enjoyed her short escapade in Honduras, but she had the luxury of going home the next day. She will share with her friends a false picture of the strike and of life in Honduras. This tourist impression of life in a Third World country is dangerous. There is so much to love and even admire about El Paraíso, but the reality is that the vast majority of people here and throughout Honduras are dirt poor and live an extremely difficult life. The strikes do nothing to improve this. Now, where's my Advil?

Can I Get a Light, Please?

The following is an actual phone conversation between Cristina and the El Paraíso Electric Company (EPEC). As Dave Barry would say, "I'm not making this up."

EPEC: *Hello.*

Cristina: *Hello, is this the Electric Company?*

EPEC: *Yes.*

Cristina: *Ok, well I would like to report a street light that is out.*

EPEC: *Ok, where do you live?*

Cristina: *We live in Barrio Rosario.*

EPEC: *Oh, yes, we know about that light.*

Cristina: *Do you plan on fixing it?*

EPEC: *Yes, but not anytime soon. The light bulb is out.*

Cristina: *Oh, it's the light bulb. Do you think it will be fixed in a week or a month?*

EPEC: *We're not sure.*

Cristina: *You're not sure.*

EPEC: *We are out of light bulbs.*

Cristina: *The Electric Company is out of light bulbs?*

EPEC: *Yes, we have been out of light bulbs since the beginning of the year* (7 months).

Cristina (louder): *De veras!* (Spanish for what the ?%!$!). *The electric company has no light bulbs.*

EPEC: *Yes* (as if this is normal).

Cristina: (silence)

EPEC: (silence)

Cristina: *Ok, bye.*

EPEC: *Bye*

July Fourth, 2004

How does one celebrate the Fourth of July in another country? The same way one does in America: we eat! Cristina and I march into our local grocery store and buy hot dogs, potatoes, and Coca-Cola. After cooking up the hot dogs, which shrink to the size of my pinky, we enjoy them with our homemade fries and drink. We have no fireworks, so Cristina recommends we blow up roosters instead. It's tempting.

Taking in the sun on Independence Day, I contemplate what it means to be an American. Unfortunately, for many here the view of an American is based on what is seen on television and in movies. Among others, there is a different perspective. Today I'm talking to Nestor, a friend who keeps statistics for the Health Center. I am dropping by to get some information on rates of diarrhea in surrounding neighborhoods that I'm hoping will help me select the most at-risk communities. Nestor, never one to waste time on small talk, swings his chair around to face me and begins to speak. He is clearly frustrated. "I lived in the U.S. for a short time, a very short time. It's different there. You Americans believe you can do anything. You believe that you must work hard but that anything is possible. You work hard and try to fix problems."

He stands up and walks over to his desk, fingering through some papers. He picks one up and turns back towards me. "We do not do that here. We do not think we can change things. You are the only one who comes in here. How can people know where to begin to solve health problems if they never come in here to see me? It's not that they don't care, they are just indifferent. They don't believe they have the ability to change things." I sense his discourse is important, and I soak up every word. It is the first time that a Honduran, a man who loves his country very much, has spoken to me so openly. I have no reply. Nestor hands me the information I need and looks me in the eyes. "It is different in the U.S." he says, as he returns to his desk.

My day of enlightenment continues as I stop in to talk to my barber. He's a young man with a thorough knowledge of U.S. history and our founding fathers. At the end of our conversation, he looks up at me from his seat and says, "Kevin, do you believe that in the U.S. anything is possible?" "I do," I reply. He looks at me, as if pondering my response. "I think in Honduras anything is possible," he adds. Then, he looks at the ground and laughs, shaking his head back and forth. His laughter continues as he stands to greet a customer entering the room. I say goodbye and head back into the streets of El Paraíso.

Me and Cuyalí (coo-yaw-lee)

Erika continues to educate me on the terrain of El Paraíso and the reality of life in my little town. Today, she has asked me to accompany her to the school in Cuyalí, three miles north of the city, to give a talk to some fifth graders about HIV and AIDS prevention.

We hop on a bus to Cuyalí. The first thing I notice as we enter Cuyalí is the tremendous amount of garbage. After the recent rains, the roads have turned to muck. Young children run through the streets naked, covered in mud, and playing among the garbage. There are pigs, chickens, ducks, horses, mules, and cows wandering around and leaving their droppings wherever. The smell of standing water on the side of the road mixed with garbage and animal feces makes me nauseous.

When we arrive at the school, we are informed that on this day, the fifth graders will be arriving at noon. It is only 9:10, so I have plenty of time to observe. I should have closed my eyes.

At 9:10 the kids are in recess. This ends at 9:40 when the daily snack is presented. Snack time consists of a few kids drinking rice milk while most of the others throw cups at one another. The third graders decide to play a game I call, "Let's make a circle around the gringo and stare at him." It's cute, because many of the kids in the smaller communities rarely see a foreigner, and they love it when I try to pronounce their names. They laugh and jabber in Spanish and I laugh and mumble in Spanglish. It's a hot day, and at about 10:20 the third-grade teacher tells her kids it's time to return to class. Rounding up a group of cattle while riding an otter could not have been more difficult. By the time the teacher, in no hurry whatsoever, corrals her students, it is 10:50. Recess and snack have now lasted one hour and 40 minutes, for those of you keeping score at home.

From a chair outside the director's office, I look across a span of grass and observe all four classes. Unfortunately, classroom instruction mirrors recess. It is mayhem. Things get worse. At 11:00, three of the four teachers leave their classrooms and meet outside to have a little chat for the next 45 minutes. Meanwhile, I watch children climb on desks, throw backpacks, and pee on the side of the school. One kid pees directly on the sign that reads: *"Esta escuela es de nosotros. Cuidela."* ("This school belongs to all of us. Take care of it."). Every ten minutes, the second-grade teacher enters the room with a large wooden stick, bangs on the chalkboard and demands silence. This is greeted with silence, followed by more mayhem. Then it gets worse. At 11:30, the same teacher enters the classroom, dodges some kids, and grabs an article of clothing from her desk. *That's odd. It's not cold out.* She then reaches into her pocket, pulls something out, and begins to . . . sew! Yes, she is sewing. She is sewing her sweater. Sewing! At 11:45, the teachers return to their classrooms and tell the kids to clean up and go home. It has been a rigorous day. In another classroom, the fifth graders are arriving and awaiting our presentation.

As I sit outside, under a blue sky, surrounded by incredible green mountains, I'm homesick and doubting my decision to come to Honduras. If these teachers, Hondurans, either don't care or have given up, what am I doing here? I look up to the sky and ask for help. I don't want to feel this way after such a short time. In this moment, I am angry at the teachers. They represent the same teachers that just went on strike for one month, received each of their demands, and cost the kids a good chunk of their school year. I'm pissed off, and I'm sad. If this is the state of education here, where is the hope? Am I wasting my time down here? If so many Hondurans clearly don't care, then why should I?

Feeling a bit dejected, I enter a classroom of 34 fifth graders and talk to them about AIDS prevention. We discuss the definition of

HIV and AIDS, the growing number of youth contracting it, and how to protect oneself. We play a game where the kids must look at a picture and decide whether or not the person is at risk of contracting HIV. In the first picture, two adults are holding hands. The majority of the class expresses that the adults are at risk. In the next picture, a boy being bitten by a mosquito, the class unanimously votes that the boy will probably contract HIV.

I am shocked. I know AIDS education is lacking here, but when you see how much money other countries (like the United States) are spending on education campaigns, you assume there is some level of understanding. It's hard to believe that a virus that is killing millions every year is still so misunderstood.

As I start to head home, I see a group of kids kissing each other on the cheek, which is a common way to say "goodbye." One child begins joking that the kissing kids are going to give each other AIDS. Two of the fifth graders quickly correct the joking student. This makes my day.

The Plan

Given Cristina's background, she refuses to embark upon anything without analyzing the possible outcomes, and I simply can't get anything done if I don't have a long-term goal. One of the benefits of our work is the flexibility to veer from our initial assignments and, within the general guidelines of the programs, match our interests and skills with the people and projects we feel will provide results. It is an unprecedented opportunity to have the freedom to make positive change in whatever way we feel it is possible. So, over the course of the next month, we develop a strategy that we hope will have the most impact on the community during our limited time in El Paraíso.

In this first year, the plan is to present a 15-week course, which we call *"Encargado de Mi Vida"* (In Charge of My Life), to fifth and sixth graders. The course will cover communication skills, values, self-esteem, roles and stereotypes, sexuality, and HIV/AIDS prevention. We will use this opportunity to get to know the teachers and children, as well as to introduce ourselves to the community. This first phase of our project will last, if all goes well, from August until the end of the school year in November.

We decide to select three schools, one each in the communities of Cuyalí, San Juan, and Monte Cristo. We select Cuyalí and San Juan because of their poverty level and high degree of health problems in relation to the rest of El Paraíso. We choose Monte Cristo because I have met the director of the school there and am impressed with her ideas and saddened by the number of young people joining gangs and dropping out of school. In San Juan and Monte Cristo, Cristina and I will work together. Due to Cristina's obligations in other places, I will temporarily work alone in Cuyalí.

At the beginning of the new school year in February 2005, Cristina and I intend to select 12 – 15 sixth graders in each community who will have successfully completed this course. These students will form three leadership groups that we will work with for the next year and a half. Implementing activities from "Odyssey of the Mind" and ideas from friends in Peace Corps, we aspire to bring out more creativity and higher-level thinking skills than we have seen among kids in these communities or anywhere in El Paraíso.

The idea for this plan will likely be altered over the next few months. In San Juan and Cuyalí especially, children are not attending high school after sixth grade. A group of adult leaders in San Juan folded after just a couple of months. Other adults in these communities work long hours and have shown little interest in AIDS prevention training. The Health Center suffers from a lack of time and motivation in their efforts to reach communities outside the city center. Finally, we have discovered that in these communities people tend to stay. People in Cuyalí were born in Cuyalí and have no plans to leave. This is true in Monte Cristo and San Juan as well.

Therefore, we hope that by targeting children in fifth grade we will achieve several goals. For example, girls in all three communities are getting pregnant as early as 12 years old. The *"Encargado de Mi Vida"* course will provide information that they have not yet received and ideally lead to thoughts about choices and consequences. Also, many children as early as fifth grade are using drugs and joining gangs. According to teachers and community members, these problems stem from lack of adult role models, low self-esteem and boredom. We hope that by empowering youth leaders we will address these concerns in a small way. Nothing sways kids from deviance more than supportive peers.

The plan, on paper, looks good and overwhelming at the same time. Some already say we are crazy to think we can mold unruly fifth graders into a group capable of such things. I will question my thinking at times, but right now ignorance is bliss. I see this project as a wonderful challenge that seems most relevant to the situation we face in these three communities.

A Glimmer in Cuyalí

I depart the bus in Cuyalí and am relieved to see a pickup truck waiting to give me a lift to the school (usually a one-mile walk). I jump in and smile politely at the two women in the back with me. I'm heading to the school to continue working with the fifth graders. My smile quickly turns to a frown as the two women inform me that classes have been canceled for the day. I decide in my frustration to continue to the school and see what the teachers are up to. I honestly do not believe the kids have had even a full week of classes since we arrived. This can hardly be called an educational system.

As the pickup truck comes over a small hill, I see a group of kids in uniforms outside the locked gate of the school. There are about 12 of them, and I wonder what they are doing there. Then I realize they are the kids in my class. They begin jumping and cheering as we approach the school. I leap out of the pickup truck and ask them why they are hanging around the school when there are no classes. No one, it seems, had told them classes were canceled, and they decided to wait in the hope that I would arrive.

I am shocked. "Wait, you guys want to have class today?" I ask. "Yes!" they reply in a chorus. Fortunately, a group of high school kids had planned on using the building this morning, so a man arrives with keys to the school. He unlocks the fifth grade classroom and we enter. The kids are hilarious. "Okay, Kevin," says one peppy girl, "We have recess at 9:00 a.m., so I think you can give your *charla* (presentation) before recess. We will have recess, and then afterwards you can teach math and civics." I want to hug her. They direct me to the teacher's desk and help me get organized. I explain that I have to meet another group of students in a few hours and will have to leave at my usual time. They are disappointed.

I cannot believe this scenario. Classes are canceled, and 12 students wait at the school for 20 minutes to see if another teacher will arrive. They are excited that I arrive because they will have school. They want to learn. They really want to learn. As is often the case here, my emotions are mixed. I am proud of my kids, sad for their situation, and mad at the adults responsible for their education.

I spend the morning giving the kids a *charla* about HIV/AIDS prevention. A majority listens and participates. Most even take notes. Lately, I have spent much of my time trying to fight back the nagging feeling of hopelessness that seems to linger everywhere here. But in these two hours I see hope. I see intelligent young people with a desire to learn. I work only with them one day a week for a few hours, but maybe I can help them move, even if just slightly, towards their potential. As we all depart the school yard, I turn one way, the kids the other. I walk away listening to the happy shouts of young children and notice there is a little hop in my step.

Culture Night in Monte Cristo

There is no doubt that the difficult, challenging days have outnumbered the rest. However, there are certain occasions, more frequent than I probably tend to realize, when we are content where we are.

On a beautiful evening, Cristina and I walk out to Monte Cristo where some of our fifth and sixth graders are participating in the annual "Culture Night" celebration. The school is buzzing as teachers prepare the stage and mothers fix the costumes of their sons and daughters.

We are swarmed by our kids as we enter the school. A couple of boys, who seem thoroughly disinterested in virtually all of our talks, give Cristina a big hug. Our kids hug us, kiss us on the cheeks, and thank us for coming. Alex, an intelligent fifth grader, brings us over to meet his father. We are always excited to meet the parents of our kids as our attempts to organize meetings with them have proven fruitless.

Alex's dad, Raphael, gives me a firm handshake and asks about our work with his son. He has never heard of Peace Corps, nor did he have much interest. He is, to our delight, just excited someone is trying to help his son. Raphael works in the town of Danlí, one of hundreds of people in El Paraíso who work in the cigar factories. He works long hours every day, meaning he rarely sees his son. Monte Cristo can be a rough place, especially for young boys. The membership in gangs is increasing and drug use becoming more commonplace. Teenage pregnancy, like everywhere in Honduras, is prevalent. Raphael and his wife must work long hours just to get by. "I want to be a part of my son's life, but I work all day. Sometimes I try to leave early to come to meetings at the school. I worry about what he does when I'm not around," says Raphael.

According to Raphael, he has seen a change in his son lately. "He is more mature." He thanks us for helping his son, and gives us some undeserved credit. To me, there is no question as to why Alex is maturing and trying to stay out of the things that will harm his bright future: He has a dad who cares.

Culture night begins, and we settle in. We enjoy the cool evening breeze, breathe in the fresh mountain air, and just relish in the sounds of people having fun. Everything about this night is what I love so much about Honduras and the people who live here. Although the sound system falters, the stage is too small, the kids forget their lines and their dances, and stray dogs walk on stage, everyone has a great time. People laugh, they eat, they sing, and they cheer for their kids. Nothing could have ruined this night, as Hondurans know how to enjoy themselves and not worry about the little things that go wrong. It is a wonderful evening.

Carlos' Gift

One night in October, Cristina and I head over to the *Casa de la Cultura* for an evening event organized by Carlos. In front of about 40 people from the community, different groups in El Paraíso dance, sing, and play their instruments. It is a wonderful night of good entertainment. Recently, Nagisa, a volunteer from JICA (Japan's equivalent of the Peace Corps) arrived. She is an extremely talented young woman with a beautiful voice and a gift for playing piano. She has given Carlos new energy since her arrival. The evening will conclude with Carlos singing, accompanied by Nagisa on the piano. It is an opera piece, and Carlos, about 5'10" and 140 pounds, begins. As his voice booms throughout the *Casa de la Cultura*, the audience is silent, all eyes transfixed on Carlos. He bends and raises his body, extends his arms, the powerful, inspiring words exploding from his small frame.

Like everyone else in the room, I am moved and in awe of this person before me. Carlos holds the final word of the song in a booming voice and then, suddenly, he is done. There is no applause, only a collective exhale from 40 people who know they have just witnessed something very special. People begin looking around the room as if to ask, "Did you just hear that?" Then, the place erupts. People are on their feet, laughing and clapping in a standing ovation.

I am convinced that in another place, Carlos would be famous. He would be playing in front of large crowds of rich and influential people, and his name would be known by many. He is passionate about music, art, dance, and more. He is dedicated to the people of his community. Whether due to lack of opportunity or choice, Carlos stays and performs in front of 40 people on a Friday night in a quiet town that is not always aware of his gift; and in this moment, Carlos has brought his vision of what El Paraíso ought to be, into reality.

Welcome to San Juan

This morning, Cristina and I grab our bags and head up the hill to work with the students at the school in San Juan. It is a small village nestled among rolling green hills and surrounded by plush mountains springing with a variety of tree and plant life. A light fog rolls calmly through, finally giving way to the hot Honduran sun.

San Juan is a fascinating place to behold. The houses are small, roughly built structures, mostly with dirt floors and leaky roofs. But I can't help but marvel at the way the houses roll with the countryside. Some homes jut out from the sides of hills, and you are sure that a little rain and a breeze would wash them away. There is no logic to the winding and climbing dirt roads that provide treacherous routes of transportation for old cars, bikes, and horses alike. Heavy rains take a monthly toll on the eroding roads, making them impassable at times. I imagine the view from above San Juan would make a picturesque painting or postcard: this rugged little community nestled amidst Honduras' natural beauty.

For all of its natural beauty, however, San Juan is a community with so many problems that I wonder if it would be easier to level the place and start over.

Once at the Health Center, Nestor showed me a graph of health problems in communities surrounding El Paraíso. San Juan topped the list. Yearly, children die from such preventable sicknesses as diarrhea and respiratory ailments. Sickness spreads quickly in San Juan, due in no small part to the horrible sanitary conditions. San Juan has no raw sewage water waste system, so people use latrines when nature calls. Or, at least in theory, they use latrines. Due to the high ground water elevation, latrines can't be built very deep. As a result, many of the latrines are full, and digging new ones won't solve the problem. The Honduras Red Cross recently scrapped a program in San Juan to build 40 new latrines for this very reason. The result is a very messy, unsanitary situation, making the spread of sickness inevitable.

With the sun beating down on the dusty road, we jump out of the way of pickup trucks making their way down the mountain and into town. My blue hat is brown by the time we reach the metal red door that is the entrance to the school. A few days ago, we met with the director of the school and received her permission to work with the fifth and sixth graders once a week. As the door swings open, we enter onto a sidewalk. To the right is a long building with a tile roof, separated into five classrooms painted in reds and greens. Bars cover the windows. There are no screens. Since the temperature here never gets too hot or too cold, most classrooms we have seen are open like this. To our left are some concrete steps that lead down to the basketball court which is used exclusively to play a form of street soccer. There is no extra classroom available, so this is where we work with the kids. Behind the classrooms are the latrines and a grassy area. The entire grounds are surrounded by a high concrete wall topped off with thick barbed wire. The only entrance is the red door that is supposed to remain locked. Why so much security? We will soon find out the reason.

The classrooms overlooking the court are loud and unruly, and we must speak loudly to be heard. Maintaining our students' attention is a struggle. After a few minutes the kids settle down and start participating. Things are going smoothly when suddenly several children start to move around--a couple even look nervous. I tell them to please sit down, oblivious to why they are acting so strange. Then, a girl screams and moves away from our group. Cristina grabs my arm and says quite calmly, "Turn around." Behind us and approaching the group is a man dressed only in his underwear and waving a rather large branch of a tree. He has walked right through the open red door. We look up from the basketball court toward the classrooms and are alarmed to see the teachers locking their doors. The director (I use this term loosely) looks at Cristina and me through a classroom with an expression that seems to say, "Good luck. You're on your own."

We manage to keep our kids in a circle, but they are scared. I'm not sure how I feel. Not surprisingly, I've never been in such a situation. As the man moves closer to our group, I begin to formulate my plan. My first goal will be to get the branch out of his hand. Before I can think much further, one of the male teachers bursts out of his classroom and proceeds to chase the intruder around the school. Then, Cristina and I turn to our kids and speak words one would never imagine speaking: "Kids, please try to ignore the half-naked man with the big stick who is approaching us as well as the teacher currently chasing him with a broom." In a matter of seconds, the trespasser is chased away, and we are able to continue. Surely, next week will go better.

Next Week

A week later, we settle in for our next meeting in San Juan. The kids gather quietly outside in a circle on the basketball court when a minor disturbance occurs. From the classrooms we hear screams, and suddenly over a hundred children come pouring out of the rooms as the classrooms become engulfed in smoke. Cristina and I don't even flinch. After all, this is San Juan. In San Juan, as in many communities in Honduras, trash is burned. The director of the school apparently felt it would be a good idea to burn the school's trash next to the building, during school hours, and under the supervision of one fourth-grader. The fire got out of hand, and the entire school is now covered in smoke.

After the smoke clears, literally, we attempt to get back to work. However, I cannot speak over the noise coming out of the other classrooms. I am livid at this point, and the kids can tell. I decide to try to talk to the teachers. I approach one of the classrooms and immediately discover the problem. In the room are 40 unattended third graders. Three of the five teachers, annoyed by the smoke, are in the director's office taking a breather while their kids are locked in the rooms!

I nearly lose what little sanity I have left. Cristina is looking at me with slight panic in her eyes. *What's Kevin about to do?* I maintain my composure, and Cristina and I make a decision. We tell the kids that we are leaving for the day and will return when we have found a new place to meet. We cannot teach and they cannot learn in this environment, we explain. This is a difficult decision to make, and a few of the kids are upset about it. Most don't understand. To them, this is a normal school day.

Cristina and I walk the dusty roads of San Juan in silence. Nothing it seems is going right. We haven't been in El Paraíso long, but we are already wondering if we should even be here. It seems so pointless sometimes. "Let's go see Esmeralda," I say quietly to Cristina.

Esmeralda's house sits off of a rugged road in San Juan. A large gate opens to a steep stairway leading to her house. It's fitting to me that her house sits high above the road, because to Cristina and me she is an Angel.

The first time we met Esmeralda, she was in jeans and a T-shirt working hard to clean up the yard around the small Catholic church in San Juan. She walked over to us, with two other women, and introduced herself. Esmeralda is a slender, young woman with dark skin, dark eyes and a smile that stretches across her face. It's that smile that I will never forget. She and her friends, members of a volunteer group in San Juan, walked us around the church and through some of the streets. Esmeralda shared with us the projects that she and her friends hoped to implement in the future. Nearly all of the projects dealt with beautifying San Juan. Esmeralda wants people to take pride in their small community, and she wants to witness the change.

As soon as we see her smiling face, we begin to feel better. She brings us some coffee as we explain our difficulties. Nothing fazes Esmeralda. Where there is a problem, there is a solution. She says we may be able to use the small Catholic church for our *charlas*. Inexplicably, within five minutes of suggesting this idea, the director of the church stops by her house to visit. The director, without hesitation, gives us permission to use the church every Monday morning. As Cristina and I wave goodbye to Esmeralda, we look at each other with curious grins. What led us to go see Esmeralda? Was it merely coincidence that this chain of events took place, or was it more than that? We decide to head back to the school to share the good news.

Fittingly, the red door to the school is locked. That would have been much more useful to us a week ago. I push these negative thoughts to the back of my head where they belong. Cristina sticks her head through the small opening in the door and gets the attention of a second grader in a crowded classroom with no teacher in sight. The precious little girl smiles and walks towards her classroom door. She cannot, however, let us in the school. She is locked in her classroom.

Meet the Parents – San Juan

For the next few weeks, we successfully hold our meetings at the church, which is conveniently located just down the road from the school. After working with the kids (about 75 in total) for six weeks, we arrange to have a meeting with the parents. We are moving into a series of *charlas* on sexuality and AIDS prevention. In these *charlas* we will talk about some sensitive and controversial issues, primarily the use of a condom.

We schedule the meeting at 4 p.m. and arrive at 5 p.m., the *Hora Hondureña*, ("Honduran Hour"). The *Hora Hondureña* is the actual meeting start time which, as we have learned, is always at least one hour later than the scheduled start time of a meeting. I've yet to understand how or why this came to be, and it was one of the most difficult aspects of Honduran culture to accept. We wait a little longer and eventually six people arrive. Three are mothers of our students along with the sixth-grade teacher. Also arriving is the cousin of one of our students and the sister of another. They are young women representing their mothers at the meeting.

Cristina and I introduce ourselves, and talk about the *charlas* we've been giving and how much we enjoy working with the kids. Things are rolling along just fine until it is time to explain the topic of the final *charla* we will present in about a month. I explain that we will discuss AIDS prevention. Of course, the parents can tell us if they do not want their child to attend. Abstinence and fidelity will be presented as the most effective ways to protect oneself from the deadly virus. Then I tell the group that we will discuss the condom as a means of prevention and will do a demonstration involving a condom and a . . . cucumber.

Silence. Absolute silence. The two younger women in the front row (sister and cousin) are trying to stifle their giggles. The sixth-grade teacher and one mother nod approvingly. Another mother blushes, covers her face with her hand and giggles. The oldest mother simply stares. She places one hand on her forehead, slouches in her chair, puts her other hand on her stomach and appears ready to pass out. I watch her closely, ready to run and get help. She slowly raises her hand. "Excuse me," she says quietly. "I really don't think we should be discussing things like this with our kids." She stares at the ceiling appearing ready to lose her lunch. "Why can't you just talk to them about the importance of work, obedience, and responsibility?"

I'm grateful for her honesty, and I look at Cristina for some help on how to best explain ourselves. Before either one of us can say a word, the sixth-grade teacher leans forward in her chair. "I want to say something," she says. Thank goodness. For the past six weeks, I haven't been sure this teacher has had any interest or knowledge of what we have been doing with her students. Now it appears she is about to defend us. She turns to face the reluctant mother. "The kids trust these two," she says, pointing an arm in our direction. She now leans farther forward, drawing herself closer to the mother. "My kids, these sixth graders, are having sex right now." A couple of members of the group look out the window towards their homes. *Right now?* The elder mother fans herself. She groans and grabs her head. "If your kids don't learn this stuff here, then who is going to teach them? They will learn it on the streets or from television. We need to take advantage of these two people right here." Then another mother jumps in. She explains that all mothers in San Juan are afraid to talk about these things with their kids and someone has to do it. Should it be us or them? The group agrees they would rather it be us. For the next 15 minutes, Cristina and I say little. It is wonderful watching Honduran family members throw the issues on the table and discuss them. As they will be the first to admit, discussing sex is taboo. It just doesn't happen.

In San Juan, where sex and drugs are prevalent among so many youth, the parents are scared. At the end of the meeting, the elder mother approaches Cristina and me. She gives each of us a hug and a kiss on the cheek and says, "Thank you." I'm not sure what she is thanking us for, but it is clear in her face that she is happy we are here. I'm humbled by her gesture and in awe of a San Juan community that has welcomed us so graciously and entrusted us with its most precious resource: the children.

Taking the Bus – Cuyalí

Cuyalí sits off the main road between El Paraíso and the larger northern town of Danlí. Each day hundreds of people travel back and forth between these two towns. Like rush hour in the U.S., the morning and afternoon bus rides are the busiest. I detest riding the bus in El Paraíso. Most of them are old school buses from the United States that were no longer deemed usable. They are exhaust-blowing vehicles with uncomfortable seats driven for the most part by people with absolutely no concept of safety. There is no limit on the number of riders allowed, so I imagine sardines have more room to wiggle than I do on most trips.

I wait at the bus stop with about 15 fellow riders. The bus never stops in the same place, so my first goal is to stand along the sidewalk at the point where I believe the door will open when the bus comes to a stop. Next, I evaluate my fellow riders. Who looks like a pusher? Who do I not want to anger? When the bus stops, it will be a mad dash to the door. The elderly and disabled receive no priority or consideration. It is every man, woman, and child for himself or herself. My competition for a possible remaining seat on the bus includes several elderly women off to sell goods in Danlí, a few high school students in uniforms, and some young men off to work. It's a fight I can't win without sacrificing moral conduct, so I accept that unless the bus door stops directly in front of me, the odds of gaining a seat are small.

The yellow bullet comes peeling around the corner, and I position myself strategically. The driver is grinding the gears while his

61

assistant, hanging out the open door, is assessing the situation. *Please stop in front of me. Please stop in front of me.* I take a step back as the bus approaches the curb. The open door approaches and scoots by, resting about 15 feet from where I am standing. I watch helplessly as the mad rush ensues. I wait at the back of the "line" and board. No seats.

As more people board at each stop, I am shuffled to the back. Soon, my back is against the rear emergency door, and I literally have no room to move. The aisle is a mass of two single file lines. It's hot, and I'm feeling claustrophobic. There is a mumbling around me as the driver continues to pile in more riders. Another bus will be coming behind us in just minutes, so this uncomfortable and dangerous situation is completely unnecessary yet financially lucrative for the driver. I can't see out the window, but I'm sure we are a few minutes from the stop for Cuyalí. The assistant is now in the back of the bus collecting money. I hand him two *Lempiras* and tell him I will need to get off at Cuyalí. "You need to get to the front and tell the driver," he says, never looking up. With the music from the bus sound system blaring reggaeton music (a genre of dance music, popular in Latin America, influenced by Jamaican reggae, and absolutely mind-numbing to me) in my ear, I attempt to explain, nearly yelling, to the assistant, that this is impossible. He never looks at me and just points to the front. In this moment, I imagine an elephant would have an easier time squeezing into a Porta Potty than I have of working my way to the front in time. I'm not happy.

I push and squeeze, grateful at this time for the ten pounds I've lost due to a steady diet of beans and tortillas and a lot of walking. It takes me nearly five minutes to reach the front. At this point, I realize I've missed my stop, but I decide to play dumb. "Cuyalí please," I say to the driver. He looks at me, looks at the road, and mumbles something while pointing to the back of the bus. This is his way of telling me that Cuyalí is somewhere back there. Again I say, "Cuyalí please." This time I'm louder, and now my fellow sardines are taking notice. "You missed it," he says.

I'm hot, uncomfortable, and all-around annoyed that Hondurans have to endure this transportation disaster. "I know I missed it," I say in a loud voice that has some fellow riders snickering. *Yeah,* I'm thinking in my head, *I'll stick up for us. Soon, my fellow riders will rally behind me as we stick it to the driver who has packed us into this sauna. I will be a hero.* I continue. "I was in the back of the bus yelling, 'Cuyalí,' but you couldn't hear me because the radio is blasting." I'm on a roll and those around me are enjoying this. "No one on this bus can move, and it was impossible for me to get up here in time." I look around expecting to see nodding heads and others ready to jump to my defense. No. Mostly, people are just laughing at me. Nobody backed me up or even appeared to feel slightly sorry for me. It's as if they are all saying, "Welcome to our daily world. Sit down and deal with it."

The driver, unfazed by my tirade, mumbles something else and then sticks half of his body out the window. He begins to wave and yell frantically. A bus heading in the opposite direction brakes and pulls over. The driver of my bus does the same and tells me to board the bus across the street that is heading towards Cuyalí. I descend the steps slowly, feeling like a losing game show contestant and lumber across the highway. As I board my new bus, I notice all eyes are on me, the gringo who missed his stop. I want to plead my case, but there is no point.

As I ride towards Cuyalí, I try to make sense of the events. Hondurans rarely ever, at least noticeably, get angry. They never seem to demand anything of anyone. They move through the day accepting whatever comes along, frustrated but not angry. Sometimes, I have incredible admiration for this, and other days it drives me crazy. I'm shaking my head at all of this when the assistant on the bus approaches me. "Two *Lempiras,*" he says. I hand over the money and get comfortable in my seat. "Cuyalí please."

What Are You Smoking?

Cristina has been spending her days working with the Tourism Commission, a group of people attempting to bring visitors to El Paraíso. The commission has identified a few possible ideas. One is tours of a local cigar factory. Today we are heading out to Monte Cristo to tour the factory. A few members take the bus. We choose to walk. I'm still embarrassed about my last bus journey.

Approaching Monte Cristo, Cristina and I see the factory. Many of the parents of the children with whom we work are employed behind those windowless walls. In fact, most of Monte Cristo works there. Employment at the factory is highly sought after and considered one of the better jobs in El Paraíso. We meet up with other members of the commission and head inside.

The manager of the plant greets us in a nice little office that smells of tobacco. He has a large cigar dangling from his smiling mouth as he announces the beginning of the tour. As our tour leader opens a small brown door, I suddenly realize how the kids in *The Lion, the Witch and the Wardrobe* felt when they emerged from closet into snow-filled Narnia. It is another world. In front of us, in an enormous room that is at least 50 yards wide and 100 yards long, are perfect rows of brown wooden tables and chairs. It's extremely hot, and the whirling ceiling fans help only a little. Seated at the tables are men and women, young and old, wrapping tobacco to make cigars. The plant employs over 600 people. As the manager explains the scene, only a few of the employees look up. It's an incredible sight. They are focused. They are focused on wrapping and cutting at an amazing

64

pace. It's like a film moving at double speed. The employees work feverishly and have no time to look at visitors or chat if they want to maximize their own profit.

I direct my attention to the manager who explains employees are paid based on production. A normal work day is 6 a.m. to 4 p.m. Anyone working longer than this, the manager adds with a big smile, is paid double for every cigar made beyond the first ten hours. He states that employees may make up to 5,000 Lempiras a month ($280). This is a good salary in El Paraíso. I decide to do some investigating myself and wander into the swarm of humanity. Cristina and I speak with three individuals of varying ages and find that they can each make between 250 and 300 cigars a day. They are paid 30 *Lempiras* ($1.70) for every 100 cigars made—that's roughly $4.75 a day. They work ten hours Monday thru Friday plus six hours on Saturday. I'm tired just listening to this. In one month, they make roughly $93 to $112, and I'm now wondering where the manager came up with $280. The hourly wage is 40 to 50 cents. Staring into the eager and friendly faces of these hard-working men and women, hands and fingernails black from rolling tobacco, I realize that I will never have reason to complain about my next job. No time to ponder this. It's on to the next room. *What could possibly be behind door number two?*

From the warehouse we enter a room that is equally long but much narrower. The smell of tobacco is stronger in here. There are roughly 50 women working in this room, all standing and stacking large tobacco leaves. In fact, there are no chairs at the work stations, meaning the women must stand most of the day. It doesn't take long for me to notice that several of the women are pregnant. I have no idea what the health implications are for an adult, much less a fetus, inhaling tobacco all day long in this form. I imagine it can't be good. Within minutes my nose is burning, and I'm beginning to cough. Cristina nudges me. She's feeling the same way and wants to get out of the room. That sounds good to me, but I'm afraid of what lies around the corner. The manager pats my back and continues his presentation. This room employs only females because only women are qualified for this specific job. *Lucky them.* Apparently women are better able to see the colors in the tobacco leaves and therefore separate them correctly. According to our guide, most are single mothers.

The cigar factory does not produce a single cigar that is sold in Honduras. They are exported to the United States and other countries. I notice that the majority of the cigars in the warehouse will be sold under a name with which I'm familiar (later, the manager tells me that approximately 60 percent of the cigars are made for this company). There are high-end cigars and those you can find cheap at 7-11. At one point, the manager offers a member of our group a cigar that sells for $7 in the U.S. That number now sounds outrageous.

In the U.S., I often enter a store, buy a product, and never have a clue where it comes from or who is making it. I don't know the people or the conditions in which they are working. Maybe, as is the case here, I just don't want to know. I'm not judging the owners of the factory. That debate is too complicated. The fact remains that many, if not all of the employees in the factory, are grateful to have a job. If the plant closed tomorrow, 600 people would be unemployed in a town where many are looking for a job, any job. They receive more money working in the factory than they would doing just about anything else. You're not happy working at the plant? No problem, there are plenty of others eagerly waiting to take your place. These workers make a good wage in comparison to others in town. Yet they live in extreme poverty--just less extreme, I guess.

Cristina and I begin our walk back to El Paraíso. We feel depressed about what we have witnessed. How can people work in these conditions every day? Is it survival? Just before we left the plant, Cristina was talking to a woman who had been working there for 14 years. She was placing a $7 cigar into a plastic tube. She looked up at Cristina and said, "I like working here. It's quiet and peaceful."

How Would the Brady's React?

It's another beautiful, clear, crisp evening in El Paraíso. I'm sitting in the living room in my plastic chair, enjoying a quiet night with a good book, when a few words from my lovely wife in the next room shatter my peaceful world. "Oh my God! That is the biggest spider I have ever seeeeen!" I know that is my cue to come look. I don't want to move but understand that it is my job to kill such things. *Really, how big could this spider be?* I roll my eyes, and wander into the wash room. I stop dead in my tracks. It cannot be. Please, no. Sitting ever so silently in the upper corner of the wall is a gigantic . . . it's difficult for me to even say . . . *tarantula!* I've never seen one of these in real life. In fact, my only experience was seeing one on an episode of *The Brady Bunch*. The thing is big, brown, and hairy, and I want to run away. I try to stay calm. Cristina is staring at me, then the creature. She's clearly waiting for me to take action. I'm frozen. How can I kill this thing without actually getting any closer than I am right now?

Fortunately (I can't believe I'm saying this), about a month ago our house was invaded by ants. I bought a can of a high-powered chemical spray that is probably illegal in most countries. It did the trick. I run into the kitchen and arm myself. I approach the beast carefully, not wanting to startle him (which in turn would cause me to pee my pants). I raise my weapon and unleash a chemical fury, hoping not to miss. The creature falls from the wall with a thud and scurries near my feet. I dance around, spraying and jumping. It's chaos. Cristina, who usually complains that I spray too much of the chemical, is yelling, "Spray it more, spray it more ... spraaaayyy it!" I oblige.

Finally, the creature slows to a halt. I return to my plastic chair, empty spray can in hand. Cristina pats her hero on the back. Our house will reek of the chemical for a week, but Cristina won't mind.

A month later my mother-in-law mails us a newspaper article that states tarantulas make good pets. No thanks.

You'll Have to Wait Your Turn, Mr. President

Israel is a friend of mine who lives down the street. In El Paraíso everyone lives down the street. He's a vibrant husband and father of two wonderful young women. He's full of energy and a big fan of U.S. politics. He has become my Honduran expert on current events. It's election time in the U.S., and John Kerry and incumbent George Bush have been participating in internationally televised debates that I've yet to see. After each of these debates, I head over to Israel's house for an update. He gives me a one-of-a-kind commentary that I trust more than any talking head on television.

Tonight he is excited. Israel seems to prefer Kerry although he doesn't think too highly of either one. He is bouncing around his living room, from one chair to the other, reenacting the highlights of the most recent debate. Israel loves democracy and doesn't believe Honduras has one. So, when he sees two candidates forced to answer tough questions in front of the entire nation, he gets wound up. His favorite moment came when the moderator interrupted George Bush to tell him it was not his turn to speak. The fact that an ordinary citizen can tell the President of the United States that he has to wait his turn gets Israel very excited. He loves the U.S. for this.

The Curse of the Bambino and El Paraíso

The Boston Red Sox just won the World Series. I sit at home, frantically revising my two-year plan. My expectations are higher now. The Red Sox are world champions. Suddenly, anything is possible!

"Today We Kill the Chickens"

We have come to expect that just about anything can cancel our *charlas* on any given day. While still frustrating, we have come to accept this as part of life here. We arrive at the school in Monte Cristo a little after 7 a.m., and the kids are especially excited. They are running around, seemingly preparing for something. We dodge and weave our way through a sea of children and walk back to the room where we work. Just outside our room things are especially hectic, and we have that familiar feeling that something is about to interrupt our plans. A very peppy fourth grader skips by, and we ask her what is going on. She stops, looks at me with a big smile, and says in her most chipper voice, "Today we kill the chickens!"

It's true. The school is participating in an experimental chicken raising project, and the day has come to kill, clean, and prepare the chickens for sale. It's a very relevant project. The director tries to convince us that we can still present the *charla*, that the project will not interrupt our plans. Just then a group of kids run by, headless chickens in hand, on their way to pluck the feathers. We'll come back next week.

They Need to Know

The day has finally arrived, one that I have been dreading since Cristina and I began our 15-week course on sexuality and AIDS prevention. It is time for the condom demonstration. Cuyalí is the site of the first *charla* on how to use a condom, and I am nervous. I feel I have bonded with the kids recently, so I am not as terrified as I might have been. Despite the fact I have come to grips with the necessity of giving this information to my kids, the thought of teaching 10-, 11-, and 12-year-olds how to use a condom still seems crazy. The statistics reveal that boys in Honduras have their first sexual encounter by age 11 and girls by age 12. This information could save their lives and not a single parent has objected to our providing it. I arrive in Cuyalí, equipped with a dozen condoms and a wooden dildo.

In Honduras, many men refuse to wear condoms. A fellow volunteer, who dedicated much of his two years to getting men to wear condoms, admitted near the end of his service that he didn't know if any of the men he had worked with wore a condom on a regular basis when having sex. Many who refuse to wear a condom do so because of the reduced feeling of pleasure that is a result. Others can't afford condoms and don't want to go to the Health Center in El Paraíso, which is located rather far from many communities and has a large supply available free of charge.

If a man does not want to wear a condom, often the woman is afraid to argue. She will accept it. There are many reasons for this. First, according to a recent newspaper article, Honduras is the most machismo country in Central America. Women are hardly seen as equal and, in many places, remain in a position of service to the men. Second, a woman fears that asking her boyfriend or husband to wear a condom indicates that either she doesn't trust him or that she has been sleeping around with other men. So, despite the risk of death from AIDS, a woman will rarely demand her partner use a condom. This must change.

The boys are first, and I am fairly certain at least one boy in my group is having sex. I explain where condoms are available, how to store one safely, and how to read the expiration date on the wrapper. Then, I reach into my bag and pull out the wooden dildo. The group loses it. They are laughing so hard, it takes me a solid five minutes for them to gather themselves and focus. Once they settle down, I am impressed. The boys are like deer in headlights as I show them the proper way to put on a condom. They even ask questions. One boy volunteers to try and successfully puts the condom on the dildo with the focus of an engineer. I am proud of them.

Then, it is the girls' turn. All fifteen of them pile out of the classroom, running towards the small circle of chairs we've been using as our gathering place in the middle of the school's field. They enjoy these sessions together and often speak more freely than the boys. I am nervous. I explain that today they will be learning how to correctly use a condom.

As the girls anxiously wait for me to begin, I first pull out a wrapped condom and repeat exactly what I said to the boys. Then, I reach into my bag and pull out the dildo. The reaction? Some girls gasp, others giggle, and two flat-out refuse to look at it. They cover their eyes and look away.

I proceed with the demonstration, and soon all eyes are fixed on me. They watch intently as I explain how to put it on properly and what the male must do immediately after ejaculation occurs. Then I ask for volunteers to put a condom on the dildo. Eight girls practice while the others watch. One girl begins, and while putting the condom on, forgets to squeeze the tip to prevent air from entering. She is bombarded by six girls, screaming, "The tip, put pressure on the tip!

There's air! There's air!" I can only hope they will be this forceful one day, if necessary, with their partner.

As we finish the *charla*, I grab my camera to take a picture. This is the last *charla* of the school year, and I want a group photo. They all gather around me, and I reach my arms around as many as I can.

I don't know if any of them will ever use the information they have just received. Looking into their happy, innocent faces, I am worried for what the future holds for them. They are an amazing group of young people, and I feel better knowing that at least they have this knowledge that could one day save their lives.

Election 2004

I know the 2004 U.S. Presidential Election will be historic, so once again I call on my good friend Israel. On Tuesday night, November 2, Israel, Cristina and I spend several hours watching the incoming results. As a citizen living abroad, the U.S. seems to be a very angry, divided country. The results, regardless of who wins, will leave many furious. Perhaps I am lucky to be far away on this day. Watching with Israel, who is fascinated with U.S. politics, I find myself enjoying the evening immensely, focusing on the beauty of democracy in action. Israel watches as each state turns red or blue. "Why does Georgia always vote Republican?" he asks, as CNN Español flashes the final count. He pulls out a book he owns, from 1970, that explains the Electoral College. As CNN updates the electoral votes, Israel immediately calculates how many more each candidate needs to win. Bush wins Florida. Kerry wins Pennsylvania, and now all eyes are focused on Ohio not just in the U.S., but around the world. "Experts" from every station and media outlet are chiming in on whom Ohio will elect. But, in truth, they have no idea. The citizens of Ohio, one state among 50, will make the decision. I am taking all of this in. Our Founding Fathers were brilliant. For all of the problems the U.S. must face within and outside its borders, for all of the lack of faith I often have in politicians, watching the election process makes me as proud as I have ever been to be an American.

Bush is up by 130,000 votes in Ohio, with 88 percent of the precincts reporting. Israel, who I have now discovered is a math whiz, quickly punches some numbers in his head. "Oh, there are still a bunch of votes left to count. Wow!" We make it to midnight and decide we will have to wait until tomorrow to find out what happens. Cristina and I walk home through the quiet streets of El Paraíso. My mind drifts home, and I can't help but feel good. The U.S. truly is a special place.

Pass the Buck

We arrive in Monte Cristo to give our *charla* on how to use a condom. The fifth and sixth grade teachers seem surprised to see us. We have been coming every Thursday at the same time for the past three months. They look at each other, shrug their shoulders, and explain that there is no time to give our *charla* today. The kids are practicing the National Anthem. The National Anthem in Honduras is seven verses, and memorization of the hymn is a requirement for passing sixth grade. In a country where most of the kids we work with have trouble with reading, basic math, and all writing skills, this requirement seems a bit overboard. In addition, our *charlas* have been interrupted four times in the last seven weeks. Cristina will have none of it.

We offer solutions, but the teachers will not budge. There just isn't time, they say. I am ready to go, but Cristina is not. She looks at me and says softly, "We are not leaving. This *charla* is too important." She turns back towards the teachers. "Okay, today we are giving the *charla* on how to use a condom and plan on showing the kids the proper way to use it. We explained this *charla* to you both before, so we'll just give you the condoms and the dildo, and you can give them the *charla*."

As Cristina starts to reach into my bag to get the condoms, the two teachers react as if there is a spider at their feet: They hop around, scratch their heads, look at each other, shoot a glance at Cristina, and huddle together. After a brief moment, they break the huddle, see Cristina fishing out the condoms, and one teacher blurts out, "Oh, wait. Okay, we can work this out. Why don't you guys take the sixth graders right now? How long do you need? An hour, right? Great. Okay. Then, when you're done, you can work with the fifth graders." She looks at the fifth grade teacher who is nodding his head and slightly sweating. He is in agreement. They congratulate each other on their fine plan. Cristina triumphantly leads the sixth graders to our workspace. Mission accomplished.

The "Good News"

It's Friday morning, and I arrive, as I do most Fridays, at the *Escuela Especial.* The school is located in downtown El Paraíso and primarily serves children with intellectual disabilities and autism. María Esther is the director, and I am lucky to work with her. Like every other school in El Paraíso, there is a huge lack of resources, and María is attempting to maximize the limited space. She does it magnificently.

María Esther is a very special person, like Esmeralda, Carlos, and others mentioned. She has a nearly impossible job. At times, she has eight young children with greatly varying degrees of intellectual disabilities, working in a small classroom. María has limited training and admits she needs more. If she is ever frustrated, she doesn't reveal it. María is always thinking ahead. She looks forward, believing that things will get better for her and her tiny school. There are plans for a new building that will be equipped with several classrooms. Currently, very few parents of children with disabilities send their kids to the school. There is almost no support within the community, and discrimination is a very real part of the lives of the children who attend. She believes that with another teacher and a new building, the school will expand. She has been told for more than a year that construction will begin. The site remains barren, and there is a rumor that another group may be pushing to build on the same land. María isn't losing hope. Despite the difficult circumstances, she has dedicated her life in El Paraíso to improving the lives of children with disabilities and their families.

I enter the school, receive a warm greeting from the kids, and set down my bag and basketball. On Fridays, I am in charge of physical education. I begin to talk with María, and after a minute she takes my arm and pulls me into the storage room. She is smiling and appears excited and nervous at the same time. "I have good news. I think we will be moving to the U.S. to live," she says.

I'm sure I tried to force a smile, but I don't know if it worked. I believe my exact word was "What?" María explains to me that her husband's family lives in California, and she and her husband, after many years, have just received word that they are close to receiving their visa to immigrate to the U.S. She is trying not to get too excited, but things look good. It could be a year or a month. She doesn't know.

I look around the school and at the kids. María can't leave. She is too important to these kids and to this town. I have been here six months and know that people like her are rare. The reality, one that I have tried to push back in my head, hits me again. If given the chance, most would drop everything and head to the U.S. María pumps me with questions about life in the States, and I answer with as much enthusiasm as I can muster. I wonder what will happen to María in California. Here she has a purpose, a mission. There, she will have to learn English and then take classes to be certified to teach. Her family is here. Her life will be so different. However, I am excited for her, because I see the gleam in her eye. I am excited for her children who will have the opportunity to receive a good education. I am also sad. El Paraíso can't afford to lose their María Esthers. There are too few of them.

As the last of the morning students leave, María shuts the door of the school and walks with me to the corner of the street. Later that day, I will help her husband sort through the final paperwork they must compile before securing a visa. I try to imagine El Paraíso without María. I can't and don't want to. My thoughts are selfish I imagine, but my heart is with this town. If all goes "well" for María in the next year, El Paraíso will lose a valuable resource. And, I fear, very few will ever notice, much less appreciate, what their town lost.

That Is Not Soccer

I have been coaching a girls basketball team for three months at the elementary school next to our house when the director of the school's afternoon session, Blanquita, approaches me. This Friday the school is having the annual Soccer Championship, a tournament between grades in the school. She wants to know if the basketball team, a collection of 12 girls with a passion for a sport other than soccer, would like to play a little exhibition game before the tournament. I figure this a great way to promote the sport in the school and also give my girls the opportunity to showcase their skills in front of their fellow classmates. I say, "Yes."

As we start warming up before the game, I notice that both a local radio station and the local television station are setting up. I am shocked. A few minutes later, the DJ from the local radio station starts broadcasting and approaches the court with his microphone in hand. "You are Kevin, the coach of the team?" "Yes," I say, very nervously. At this moment, I'm thinking, "Please don't ask me any more questions!" I hate being put on the spot with my unique Spanish skills.

"What is the name of the team?" Great question! Since, in reality, there are no other teams in the rest of El Paraíso to compete against, we never bothered choosing a team name. I feel like an idiot. "We don't have one," I say. There are no further questions.

I divide my girls into two teams, and they begin to play. The TV cameraman is filming, and the radio DJ is doing the play-by-play. My girls are thrilled. My best player, an aggressive youngster with a natural gift for the game, breaks free with the ball and scores a basket. The following is the play-by-play broadcast heard on the radio:

Lila has the ball, she is moving with the ball, and she shoots. She made it! It went in the . . . What do you call that thing (looking around for help)? What is the name of that thing? Oh, yes, thank you, the basket. Lila made a basket. That's a point. It is 1-0. No, wait, what? (struggling to hear someone nearby.) Oh, it is two points. A basket is two points.

Basketball is coming to El Paraíso, and everyone is confused.

That's It?

These days, when we arrive in San Juan, we just assume things will go wrong. It's a good mentality to have in a place that seems to get joy from stepping on us. So, when the fifth grade teacher tells us that a group of students from the university is here to give a *charla* on values, we are disappointed but not surprised. It seems the group showed up at 9:30 and told the director they would like to speak to all of the kids in fourth–sixth grade. So we are bumped. Cristina goes to tell Esmeralda we will not need to use the church, and I wait around to watch the *charla*. I am partially excited that a group of Honduran university students is going to speak about values. I am also leery, because they have chosen to do it in front of close to 100 students.

The *charla* begins at 9:45 with the National Anthem. Then, there is a prayer. At 9:50, a student from the university asks the kids to give examples of values. The kids give a lot of one-word answers, and the presenter appears satisfied, throws in a couple of her own words, and passes things on to the next presenter. It is 9:55. He reads a quick story, similar to "The Boy Who Cried Wolf," and asks the kids what they have learned. One kid shouts, "Don't lie." "Yes," the presenter says, "lying is bad." He then looks at his counterparts, who look satisfied with what they have seen, and promptly leaves to the applause of the kids. It is 9:58.

Then, the rest of the presenters look around at each other, as if trying to decide who is next. Surely, there is more. After a couple of glances and a few head nods, the apparent leader of the group speaks. "I hope you have learned something about values today. It is important not to lie. It is important to listen to your parents and your teachers, and do what they tell you. Are there questions?" The ten kids who were paying attention say, "No!" She thanks them for their participation. It is 10 o'clock. I say rather loudly and fortunately in English, "That's It!" A couple of heads turn and smile at me.

For the next ten minutes the group from the university takes photos with the kids. I sit to the side, feeling sick to my stomach. This group of university students had an assignment. So they showed up at San Juan to give their *charla*. The director of the school drops everything, interrupts classes, postpones our *charla*, and sends all of the fourth–sixth grade students to listen. The university students waste 15 minutes of our lives so they can complete their assignment. At no time did they display any real interest in helping the kids.

Once again, as I have grown accustomed to seeing but will never accept, children were used. The university students completed their assignment (they probably celebrated how easy it was) and then left. The director praised them for their "beautiful *charla*," and everyone clapped. However, as I would soon find out, the kids weren't fooled. Kids in Honduras are smarter than many in their own country realize.

As soon as the presenters take their last ridiculous photo, I am mobbed by 20 fifth graders. "Are you going to give the *charla* now?" they plead. I think they know the answer.

Our *charlas* are certainly not perfect. At times the kids have seemed thoroughly bored with us. Other times, they don't want to participate and have even challenged our authority on occasion. Some of our *charlas* were poorly structured and seriously bombed. Our *charlas* last between 45 minutes and one hour, are very interactive, sometimes fun, and sometimes boring. The reactions of the kids are often a mixture of boredom, excitement, annoyance, and confusion. After their experience with the university students, however, I think the kids realize, at least, that we care.

I explain with much sadness that we do not have time to give our *charla*. I promise we will return next week. They are unhappy. They beg and plead. They offer solutions to the time problem. They stomp and sigh and work themselves up into a ball of anger. The fifth-grade teacher, who, by the way, is equally as upset as the kids, comes to my defense. It is, she explains, not my fault. To my selfish satisfaction, the kids are well aware of this. They are not mad at me, as a student would later confide. They are mad at the university students. They are mad that their time has been wasted and, as a result, they will miss out on a part of the day that some of them look forward to. They know, in their own way, they have been used. This is important. I hope every kid in fourth–sixth grade remembers that *charla*. I hope someday some of them are in the university and have a similar project. I pray they will actually take the time to prepare a presentation that will help reach a group of young people so desperately in need.

Nestor's Study

As Cristina and I approach Nestor's office at the Health Center, we are greeted by a thunderous *"Hola amigos."* Nestor's booming voice accompanies a broad chest and large hands that engulf mine as we greet each other. Nestor wants to share with us some information he gathered a couple of years ago. We enter the office, and Nestor quickly realizes he has left the studies at his house. He jumps on his bike and heads home. A few minutes later, he's back.

The fact that someone from the Health Center has taken the time to complete these studies is exciting. In our time here, I have seen few studies done on El Paraíso, and they were usually completed by an outside group. In 2002, Nestor spent a year traveling within the city center and to the surrounding communities to interview people and gather information. The result is a fascinating insight into the root of the problems in our town.

A growing health problem that is very preventable, diarrhea, continues to infect and even kill young children in El Paraíso. Nestor set out to find out what people, educated and uneducated, knew about diarrhea and what they were doing to prevent it. For those less educated, Nestor wanted to measure their desire to learn about diarrhea prevention and make changes accordingly in their lives. He was a little surprised and very disappointed in what his study revealed.

In a nutshell, Nestor found that even the most educated in El Paraíso were doing very little to prevent the spread of the illness or share their knowledge with others. Perhaps saddest, Nestor found the majority (both educated and uneducated) were disinterested in learning about the causes of diarrhea and working within their community to prevent the sickness. In his conclusions, Nestor uses three different words to describe the people he interviewed. All three are synonyms for lazy.

I hope and believe Nestor is at least partially wrong, but he knows the pulse of El Paraíso better than anyone I've met here. The people, he says, are waiting for the government or an international group to come in and solve their problems. They are unwilling to work as a community to combat health issues. He found that even those he described as "agents of change" (teachers and other educated citizens) showed little or no interest in sharing information on how to prevent diarrhea. Even his own friends, Nestor said, were unwilling to help him implement his recommendations for combating the problem of diarrhea in El Paraíso.

Throughout our meeting, Nestor speaks passionately about his fellow citizens. He is angry and disappointed. "What we need, if things are going to change, are 100 Peace Corps Volunteers." No, this is not the answer. This, as Cristina points out, will only make the problem worse (a scenario that seems impossible to imagine at this point). Nestor admits that the biggest part of the problem is people here have such low self-esteem. They have accepted things the way they are and, in my view, have come to expect that eventually someone else will do something about it, whatever "it" may be.

Say it Ain't So

Cristina continues to look for ways to assist in the local government office, and a young man named Antonio has been exceptionally helpful in her attempts to do so. In charge of the Catastro Office (handling matters involving property ownership and boundaries for tax purposes) in El Paraíso, Antonio is a hard worker with a friendly demeanor and desire to do his job well. As Antonio has helped Cristina learn how things operate in the office, they have become good friends.

In the midst of a rather innocent conversation about things in El Paraíso, Antonio tells Cristina he is trying to secure a visa to work in the U.S. He is married and has a child on the way. His plan is to work for two years in the U.S., save money, and return to live a better life in El Paraíso. According to town standards, Antonio is doing quite well here. But he admits he can barely pay the bills and has no idea how he will ever afford college for his child.

Cristina listens to this and says that El Paraíso can't afford to lose some of its best people to the U.S. The dam breaks, and Antonio unloads his burden. He admits, without hesitation, that he does not work for anyone but himself and his family. He has no interest in helping the people of El Paraíso because they have no interest in helping themselves. He wants to make quick money that will go a long way to improve his family's situation. Like so many others in El Paraíso, Antonio says he does not have the willingness or the patience to work hard now for something that may or may not happen in the future. He must look out for himself and his family. Who can blame him?

Antonio is a good person and, like Nestor, he is beaten down by El Paraíso and the attitudes of the people with whom he shares this town. In the midst of all of this hopelessness are people like Nestor, Erika, Carlos, Esmeralda, and others: Those who keep trying despite the challenges. We have the luxury of returning home. They do not. The question we do not want to answer is when will they decide that the fight is no longer worth the effort.

After these two experiences with Nestor and Antonio (which happen within days of each other), Cristina and I sit quietly at our kitchen table. We speak little as we try to absorb the harsh realities. They are not a surprise, these revelations by Nestor and Antonio, but hearing the words from good people living in El Paraíso is still depressing. The wall we have been trying to climb seems to be getting taller.

Felix

Felix is four and growing up before our eyes. In our first days and months in El Paraíso, Felix sat quietly on a small step in front of his house. Every day he gave us a big wave and a loud *"Adios!"*

In almost seven months, Felix has gotten bigger and burst out of his shell. He is now seen leaving the safe haven of his step and racing up and down the street in front of our house. His favorite toy is a yellow dump truck, one that sometimes accompanies him back and forth on runs to the *pulpería* at the end of our street. Often, we hear the sound of him pushing the truck down the sidewalk, a bag of sugar for coffee in the back.

A couple of years ago, Felix showed up on the doorstep of our neighbor, Gloria, a friend of his mother. Gloria agreed to take in Felix who was suffering from severe malnutrition. He was small for his size and his hair was beginning to fall out. Today, Felix is nearly impossible to slow down. His energy wears you down, but his smile picks you up on the worst of days.

Felix is a daily visitor these days. He's not tall enough to see in our window, so he stands just below it and yells, *"Hola Gringitos!"* He refuses to knock, so he continues calling our names until we answer the door. If we tell him to wait a minute, he says, *"Rápido!"* (hurry up!). In Felix's world, everything is urgent. He is usually in a hurry to either practice his colors or acquire a balloon.

"When are we going to practice my colors?" he bellows as we open the door. We are busy these days, so we tell him we're not sure. This is not an acceptable response. After excruciatingly long conversations with Felix about what day we can play, Cristina and I realize that Felix's memory lasts about five seconds. So, now if we can't play with Felix, we say, "Maybe another day." To this, he says, "Tomorrow!" We say, "Yes, tomorrow." Then the next day we have the same exact conversation.

The balloon question poses problems. We have, on occasion, given Felix a balloon. Normally, about 20 minutes later, he is back at the door. "The balloon exploded!" he proclaims, usually with a piece of it still stuck to his shirt. We say we're sorry, but he'll have to come back another day for a balloon. We prefer not to give gifts to the children, primarily because there are so many living near us. So, in relation to Felix, Cristina has an idea.

Every Tuesday, the garbage truck passes by our house. In El Paraíso, people put their week's garbage in large sacks that the garbage men then empty into the back of a truck. There are two major problems. The first is dogs. They run rampant in the streets of El Paraíso and seem to have identified the assigned days each street receives garbage service. The first few Tuesdays I put out garbage, the dogs attacked, and I spent a good part of the morning cleaning up the mess. I countered by putting heavy rocks on the top of our sack, and that solved the problem, at least for the moment.

After emptying the sack, the garbage men, very kindly, put the sack on our front doorstep under a rock. This is to prevent the wind from blowing it away. However, the problem is not the wind. It's people. For a reason I've yet to determine, people are stealing our sack. This has presented a bit of an inconvenience and angers me as I have just conquered the dogs. Our solution: Felix.

Felix is like a neighborhood gossip, sitting on his front porch all day long watching the events of the street. So, one Tuesday morning on her way to work, Cristina asks Felix to watch our sack to make sure no dogs get in and no one steals it. Since Felix tends to forget things immediately, Cristina makes this request more in joking.

I return home before lunch to find our garbage and the sack gone. Cristina arrives home a few minutes later, and we are both frustrated. *"Hola Gringitos."* Felix is at the door. I answer and Felix says, *"El saco."* I have no idea what he is talking about. When I don't understand something, Felix's solution is to say the exact same thing louder. *"El saco!"* he yells. I'm lost. He pushes me aside, enters the house, takes Cristina's hand, and leads her down the street to his house. A moment later, he emerges triumphantly with a big smile and our red garbage sack in his hand. We are shocked.

Felix has proven to be a responsible protector of our sack. His reward is a balloon which he accepts gratefully. He, of course, wants another. "Next Tuesday," we tell him. Felix has no concept of days of the week, so now, every day, he will ask if it's garbage day. He wants to earn that balloon.

Year One in the Schools:
Challenges and Successes

It is mid-November, and Cristina and I are planning our final *charlas* for the school year. After being informed by teachers that the school year is scheduled to end December 17, we depart for a reunion with fellow Peace Corps Volunteers. We believe we will have plenty of time to finish things up when we return. When we arrive back in El Paraíso on November 22 and head to San Juan for our weekly *charla*, a teacher tells us the school year will end in four days! Apparently, things have changed.

It seems the teachers decided to forgo the final three weeks of school. According to the newspaper, nearly 9,000 teachers have not received their paychecks for nearly a year. A friend, a very good teacher, has received paychecks sporadically. So the blame for the sorry state of education in El Paraíso lies at all levels.

We run around rampant the final week and manage to administer our final exam (20 questions covering sexuality and HIV/AIDS) to most of our students. It is a fitting end to a crazy four months in the three schools.

Cuyalí
Only in Cuyalí, where I am able to finish the course two weeks early, do we have the closing *charla* we envision for the course. With the support of the fifth grade teacher, we plan a *charla* and celebration with the children and their parents on the Saturday after classes end.

There are 31 students in the class, and Cristina and I hope that six to ten of them and their parents will come. This would be a success and would be more than the number who had attended our first meeting with the parents two months ago. We prepare materials and buy a cake and drinks for 31, laughing at our optimism.

It is a beautiful afternoon in Cuyalí as we approach the gates to the school. About ten kids stand out front, waiting for our arrival. The teacher unlocks the gate, and we enter the school grounds to set up. We decide to take advantage of the weather and have the meeting outside. Cristina and I watch in amazement as more people approach the gates of the school. Happiness turns to excitement as child after child arrives, half of them accompanied by a parent.

The blue sky seems to bring the nearby green mountains to life. A fresh breeze blows through the school as kids and parents pull up a chair to join the growing group. We start counting. There are 30 children and 15 parents. I want to hug everyone.

For the next hour, we talk to the children and their parents about the future. We separate the group. Cristina works with the parents, and I take the children to a separate room to have them discuss their future aspirations. Cristina asks the parents to think about what they want for their children's futures and how they feel they can support them to reach these goals. The parents are shy, and I imagine we are asking them to share feelings and thoughts they have never discussed with their own children. The majority of parents cannot read or write. By completing fifth grade, many of the children have surpassed the educational level of their mothers and fathers. A few parents admit they are not sure how they can support the goals of their children and others speak of the challenges of trying to motivate a child who does not have the desire to study or learn. Many express concerns about the economic reality of supporting dreams of higher education. School is expensive. One mother, who makes and sells tortillas for a living, wonders how she could ever finance her child's desire to study in Tegucigalpa. She explains that many children in Cuyalí are working by age 12 or 13 just to help the family keep food on the table. The parents admit that if their child wants to attend the university, he or she will have to find a way to finance it himself.

A few minutes later, parent and child sit together in the school yard and discuss the future. They design a flower that expresses how they will work together to reach the goals of the children. Goals include finding work after high school, getting married, studying in the university, and pursuing a career. The task is a challenge, and Cristina and I sit with the parents and children to help. Thinking about the future is something very few do in El Paraíso.

As the *charla* ends, we thank the parents and express our interest to continue working with their children the following year. A mother raises her hand and says, "We want to thank you for taking the time to talk with our kids about things that many of us are nervous to discuss with them."

My mind races back to our parent meeting in San Juan. The two young women, who sat in the front row in place of their parents, were only a few years older than the siblings they were representing. As Cristina and I finished sharing the themes of the course we would be presenting to the students, the two young women looked at each other. One then looked up at Cristina with a half-smile and said, "I wish someone had talked to us about this stuff."

I wonder how many of the parents in our group in Cuyalí were thinking the same thing. I am flattered by the kind words of the mother, proud of the parents who took the time to come, and hopeful that maybe our students will be willing to tackle these difficult subjects in the future with their children.

The day is a special one. It is proof that the parents in Cuyalí care deeply about their children. The day demonstrates that when people unite, a community can and will work together to address its challenges and aspirations. In a word, the day is hope.

Cuyalí is a pleasant surprise. After a few *charlas* in horrible conditions, I had been ready to quit. I had even found another school to take its place. I don't know what kept me coming back that first month. There were no classrooms to work in, so my dedicated group of kids worked outside. During my third or fourth *charla*, the director of the school decided to have the sixth graders construct a tent next to my workspace. "Don't mind them," he said, as kids with machetes and hoes clanged away. A week later, my *charla* was interrupted by a child on a donkey, racing around the schoolyard, to the delight of the kids. The director did nothing, despite my pleas for a more suitable environment to work.

But I stayed. The two teachers I worked with were wonderful, making it clear to the students that my classes were important and to be respected. This support, in a school that did little to foster learning, was priceless. I will never forget that wonderful afternoon when a group of kids waited for me on a day when classes were canceled, just to see if I would come to give their *charla*. It is a special group that has potential. We shall see.

San Juan

What more can be said about San Juan? We endured the naked man with the stick, a small brush fire, and everything else San Juan threw at us. In the end, the experience was wonderful. Both the fifth and sixth graders in San Juan did better than expected on the test. Our last two meetings with both classes were enjoyable as the kids displayed a liking for us that had been absent before.

San Juan has grown on us, and we both feel a special connection to this small community just up the road from our house. It is a place with more problems than can be solved in our short time here, but we are nonetheless excited to see what will happen next year. We watched our group of fifth graders endure unbelievable distractions but manage to retain some of what they were taught. I want to see what these kids can do in a true learning environment, something we will try our best to create next year with the most talented of our fifth graders. It is a challenge we look forward to, but one we also understand will require the dedication of our kids.

Monte Cristo

We chose to work in Monte Cristo because the director and teachers seemed motivated. Upon our initial visits, we believed we had found the needle in the haystack, an elementary school working against the odds to educate its youth. Everyone talked a great talk. Unfortunately, this was not the case. On several occasions, classes were canceled so teachers could attend trainings in a neighboring town. No one bothered to inform us, and the kids missed more and more days of school. No surprise. Our workspace was also changed several times, and eventually we wound up teaching in an empty room that had been used for storage. Chickens ran rampant through the room and pooped everywhere. Each Thursday we arrived to the horrible odor. We would mop and sweep for 15 minutes just to try to make the room appear and smell presentable. The kids grudgingly endured the smells and particles of chicken droppings still on the floor, another credit to the amazing character of some of our children.

Janet, a nurse who lives in the community next to Monte Cristo, helped us with most of our *charlas*. She volunteered her time every Thursday morning to share her knowledge with us and the kids in Monte Cristo. She is a valuable resource and a primary reason we plan to return next school year in the hopes of molding some of the fifth graders into a group of community leaders. It will be a tall task.

A Final Thought

There are days when we put our heads down on the kitchen table and mutter, "It's hopeless." We're not proud of ourselves when these words spill out of our mouths, but it is how we feel sometimes. We have encountered obstacles we never imagined. For nearly fifteen weeks in three schools it was an uphill struggle.

The results of the final exam are mixed. To our pleasant surprise, some kids did better than we expected. But it is evident that as a group they did not learn as much as we'd hoped. Sitting at our kitchen table grading the exams, reading the names, laughing about each child's unique characteristics, and remembering the challenges each school presented, we come to one wonderful conclusion: Against all odds, in an environment totally unfit for education, and in schools hampered by lack of resources, poor facilities, educational politics, and burned-out or disinterested teachers, our kids have learned.

It is further proof that in the day-to-day struggle we become wrapped up in the day-to-day struggle. Not until we had the opportunity to take a deep breath, relax, and reflect, did we fully appreciate the small miracle our kids had accomplished. So many times we considered quitting, never fully realizing the depth of our selfishness. How can we possibly give up on kids who refuse to give up on us or the seemingly impossible position the educational system in El Paraíso has put them in?

A Kernel of Corn

Every morning and afternoon on the sidewalks of El Paraíso, young children appear carrying heavy bags of corn kernels. They take these bags to a local home that has a machine that grinds the kernels into a paste for making tortillas. Afterwards, the children return to their homes carrying the ground corn in a bucket on their heads.

One beautiful sunny afternoon, Cristina and I walk to Video Club, a small business with internet access in the center of town. On our way, we spot a young girl, no more than 10 or 11 years old, struggling with a bag of corn. The young girl's bag rips and kernels of corn begin spilling out onto the sidewalk.

Fortunately, she has another bag. She attempts to place the ripped one inside the new one. The second bag is longer than the ripped one but only slightly wider, making the transfer nearly impossible.

We watch for a second as the young girl struggles, every movement resulting in more corn spilling from the ripped bag. She is frustrated but continues. She does not yell or stomp her feet, or curse as I would have done. Instead, she simply keeps trying, displaying the unbelievable patience I have seen in so many people here.

Several people walk by, seemingly unaware of the young girl's struggles. We approach and ask, "Do you need help?"

"I am trying to get this bag in the other one," she replies in a pleading tone, obviously frustrated. I hold the good bag as she and Cristina maneuver the ripped bag inside it. The task is complete . . . or so I believe.

As Cristina and I walk away, we watch the young girl take a seat on the sidewalk and begin to pick up each kernel of corn, one by one. There are at least a hundred. We stop, sit down, and help her. As she reaches for the kernels, I notice her arms are covered in small bumps and dried scabs. I have seen this skin condition in another child in El Paraíso, and it breaks my heart. From her wrists all the way up her arms are bumps and patches of dry blood from where she has been scratching. I notice one side of her face has the bumps as well.

Together, we collect all of the kernels and deposit them in the bag. The young girl never looks up as we work. When we are done, we stand, and I say, "Bye."

She does not respond because she is not finished. She slips off the sidewalk and plants herself in the dirt along the road. I bow my head, rub my forehead and watch in silence as she begins to pick up the kernels of corn that have fallen into the dirt.

We sit back down, and for another several minutes we work until all of the kernels are in the bag. We all stand, and she says, "Thank you." She struggles to lift the heavy bag into her arms and continues on her way.

Cristina and I walk for a couple of minutes in silence. We know what the other is thinking. There is nothing to say.

"Eight. There Are Eight, Dad"

On a lazy El Paraíso afternoon, I return to the house after visiting a friend. In front of our door are two young boys, Alejandro (8) and José (6). Both have been sent from their home in San Juan to purchase kernels of corn to make tortillas. They are on their way home, taking a short break on the curb outside our house, as José tries to rearrange the heavy bag on his shoulders. Alejandro, in his bare feet and torn pants, is struggling to carry his bag and hold up his pants that evidently have a broken zipper. They smile and say hello before continuing on their way.

I enter the house and, after a few minutes, decide to head over to the post office to see if we have any mail. I walk out the door, turn the corner, and spot Alejandro and José sitting on the sidewalk, exhausted. Jose's bag has ripped and with each step kernels are falling out. They have decided to stop, rest, and figure out how to resolve the problem. The sun is beginning to go down, and they still have a 20 minute walk ahead of them. I offer to carry the ripped bag.

As we walk up to San Juan, Alejandro and José tell me about their classes in school, their favorite foods, and their favorite soccer team. When we reach the house, I walk up to the front to drop off the bag of corn. I notice one of the students we had been working with sitting out front with his sister whom I also recognize. On a small bench beside them is their father.

The father thanks me for helping his sons carry the corn and offers me a seat. For half an hour, I sit and talk with him and his daughter who is attending the high school. He tells me about his work and shows me some beautiful baskets he has been making today. His daughter tells me about her work during the day and the classes she attends at night, a very difficult task considering the high school is a forty-five minute walk from San Juan.

I notice that as we are talking, several young children are coming and going. I assume they are kids from the house next door.

"Do you have family in that house as well?" I ask, pointing to a small building a few yards away.

"No", the father replies.

"Oh," I say, a little surprised. "How many children do you have?"

The father thinks and then lets out an embarrassed laugh. He shakes his head and turns to his daughter who is not at all surprised.

She doesn't miss a beat. "Eight. There are eight, Dad."

He nods. Of course there are eight.

A Cup of Coffee? Yes!

In my brief experience, people in El Paraíso take few things seriously. However, one thing that every Paraiseño considers sacred is his or her cup of coffee. El Paraíso is a coffee town, the number three producer in the country.

When Paraiseños hand a foreigner his or her first cup of coffee, they watch with a stern face. My first time was with a friend in the home of a stranger during my first weeks in town. I was handed a small cup of black coffee and a *rosquilla*, a hard bread popular for eating with coffee. I don't normally drink coffee. However, I did not refuse the kind gesture. This one single decision, not to refuse the coffee, may have saved my future in El Paraíso.

The woman and my friend watched closely as I sipped the coffee. I nodded and smiled. It was good. I now realize that any other response may have made me an outcast in the very town where I was trying to fit in. One does not, under any circumstances, refuse a cup of coffee in El Paraíso.

Today, unfortunately, I witness a fellow Peace Corps Volunteer do just this. We are visiting Israel, a man who has a small coffee farm and believes that coffee from El Paraíso is God's greatest gift to mankind. Israel offers the volunteer a steaming mug, and she simply shakes her head and says, "No thanks."

Oh dear God! I try through quiet English and many facial gestures to get the woman to change her mind. I plead with her from across the room. No, she does not drink coffee, she says.

I'm fairly certain Israel is going to have a coronary episode. He rises up from his chair and says, "No, you have not tried coffee from El Paraíso. It is delicious. Right, Kevin?" I know there is only one correct answer. "Yes!" I exclaim, attempting to distance myself as far as possible from my fellow countryman. "I never drank coffee in the U.S.A., but I do here. It's *gooooood*," I insist, trying to convince her to change her answer. She doesn't budge.

"Who doesn't drink coffee from El Paraíso?" exclaims Israel, looking in my direction. "I don't know," I say, shrugging my shoulders and trying to look equally dumbfounded.

"Who doesn't like coffee from El Paraíso?" shouts Israel's wife as she enters the room.

Now, the poor woman is in trouble. She fumbles around as she tries to explain she doesn't like all of the caffeine and sugar in the coffee. She is on the defensive, and I watch helplessly.

Every negative comment about coffee she makes, Israel and every Paraiseño takes personally. Finally, Israel throws up his hands, looks at his wife and me in disbelief, and leaves the room. The storm has passed.

The Coffee Industry

"Every year we play Russian Roulette with the coffee harvest."
- Carlos

The coffee tree is a beautiful thing. It stands several feet tall, and its beans are green for most of the year. In November, depending on the weather and the elevation of the trees, the beans begin to turn red, and the coffee tree transforms into a colorful work of nature.

Workers climb the hills of Honduras with their baskets hooked to their chests and seek out the red beans, those ready to be picked. At the end of the day, a supervisor tallies the number of baskets filled and records the results in a notebook. One basket of coffee beans is worth 15 Lempiras ($.80). The average worker, according to a friend, can fill six baskets in a day. The best workers can fill ten or more. Once a week or every two weeks, the workers receive their pay.

After the beans are picked, they are hand-cranked through a machine (on most farms) which removes the shell and sends the beans into a concrete basin. In the large coffee plants this intricate network of concrete waterways is fascinating to see. The heavier beans (higher quality) stay at one end, and the lighter ones float to another side of the waterway. My ineptness in physics and all subjects related makes me incapable of explaining exactly how this system works, but it is impressive to watch.

Now that the beans have been separated, they are ready to be laid out and dried. Once the sun does its job, another group of workers pack the beans in large sacks and prepare them for sale to the large coffee companies in town: Every afternoon in the coffee plants around El Paraíso, one pickup truck after another rolls in the gates and drop off sacks of coffee beans.

Now the bean is ready to be roasted. This takes place in enormous contraptions that tower over El Paraíso. They look like something out of a science fiction movie and most days the foul odor of the coffee beans roasting within these monsters can be smelled around town. They pour out a continuous white smoke that smells like burning plastic and reminds you daily that you live in a coffee town.

Once dried and roasted, the coffee beans are ready to be exported and sold under a variety of brands and labels.

Coffee season lasts until February. For three months, thousands of workers, both local and from cities in both Honduras and Nicaragua, pick coffee beans on the local farms. Each morning, outside our house and around town, workers, ages eight to 60 and older, sit on the side of the road awaiting a pickup truck or tractor that will take them to the mountains. It is an amazing sight.

The temperature in November, December, and January is fairly cool, and it rains frequently. No one, however, has rain gear. Most workers wear rubber boots, but I have seen many men, women, and children wearing flip flops or nothing at all on their feet.

The work day is from about 6 a.m. to 4 p.m. Workers are hired by a farm owner and are employed until all of the coffee beans have been picked. Then the workers look for another farm to work.

The workers battle very difficult working conditions, especially if it is raining. Many of the farms, located in the mountains, have very steep hills that become muddy and slick. Even when it is not raining, I do not know how they are able to climb the hills to pick the coffee beans.

Coffee season takes precedence over everything else. Entire families work the farms. For many, the money earned during the season will sustain them, barely, for the entire year. Often attendance in the schools drops when the coffee season begins. The many children who pick beans may fill a basket or two each day.

One morning, I decide to get up especially early and watch the tractors and trucks pick up workers. I observe as men, women, and children pile dangerously into the backs. I am saddened as young children grab their baskets and hop in for hours of hard labor.

This year, the price local companies are paying farm owners for the coffee beans is twice what it was last year. This is due to a smaller crop, making the demand higher, thus raising prices. The workers, however, are being paid the same wage.

A couple of weeks later, on a trip home for Christmas, I go to the grocery store with my sister. I walk down one aisle and see the endless bags and brands of coffee. It is not about the coffee that I am thinking, but the people. Somewhere in the hills of El Paraíso, at this exact moment, a poor family is struggling up the side of a hill, reaching for and picking every coffee bean in sight. Their survival depends on it.

A Christmas Tragedy

It is December 24, 2004, and I am sitting at the kitchen table in my sister's house in Northern Virginia, enjoying the holidays with my family. My brother-in-law hands me the *Washington Post*. Buried among the national and international news is a headline from Honduras.

Yesterday, a local bus in San Pedro Sula, the industrial capital of Honduras, was traveling its normal route. Inside, were 44 local residents, returning from work and last-minute Christmas shopping. As the bus eased off the main road and onto the dirt road that would take the tired passengers home, two cars pulled up. One blocked the front of the bus, the other the back. Before anyone knew what was happening, gang members climbed out of cars and began firing into the bus, working their way methodically up and down the bus for five minutes, determined not to miss an inch. Then they entered the bus to make sure all 44 were, at the very least, shot.

On the front of the bus they left a personal note for the President of Honduras. They were not pleased with his policies, and the 44 on the bus were their message. Twenty-eight were dead, including a two year-old; sixteen were wounded.

I have lived in Honduras for only 11 months, but reading the article makes me realize just how connected to the small country I now feel. In a way, I know the 44 people on that bus. I ride with them every day. Hondurans are kind and generous. They give more than they have and endure more than I ever imagined. Now, two days before Christmas, 28 men, women, and children are massacred. It's not fair.

Homecoming, January 2005

I don't know what it feels like to be famous and probably never will. Upon our return to El Paraíso, I got a glimpse. Our neighbors welcomed us with warm greetings, food, and even a "Welcome Back" card. It seems that some people in town figured we weren't coming back. The outpouring of love and kindness is touching. Cristina and I joke that when we left our apartment in Atlanta for a two-week vacation, no one even noticed. Here, everyone asks about our trip and the welfare of our families. Even more amazingly, they are sincere in their concerns. What a wonderful way to start the new year.

Look Out the Front Door

After a celebration of the Anniversary of the *Casa de La Cultura*, Cristina and I sit at a table to enjoy the best part of any get together in Honduras: the after-meeting refreshments. We grab our food and drink and find a small table away from the crowd. Seated at our table are three friends.

Giovanni is a spirited Honduran who works for a non-profit agency in Danlí. He spends his days working on projects to improve life for people living in several poor communities surrounding El Paraíso and Danlí. I like Giovanni because he always speaks frankly of the challenges he faces. He argues that most people simply are not willing to take the steps necessary to prevent sickness and disease. Changing the habits of adults is an uphill struggle, even if the changes can improve or even save their lives, he says. Giovanni uses the examples of the *fogones mejorados* to prove his point.

In and around El Paraíso and Danlí many children are suffering from respiratory ailments. The high number can be attributed in part to *fogones*, large ovens that use wood for fuel and emit large quantities of smoke that fill the homes. Giovanni and his coworkers have been installing *fogones mejorados* (improved *fogones*) in many communities. These new *fogones* have chimneys that move the smoke out of the house and also use less wood. "Now, let's say we put a *fogón mejorado* in one home in a community," says Giovanni. "Suddenly, the family is using less wood, their house is smoke-free, and the kitchen is very clean and comfortable for cooking. So, the neighbor comes by and is in awe of the new *fogón* and its many benefits. What does she do?

110

She goes home and waits for someone to come along and build her one. She takes no initiative to improve her own life."

Seated across from Giovanni is Irene, the director of a local school who is nearing retirement. In my one visit to her home, she spoke passionately of the needs of the children and of the difficulties they encounter in their young lives. Finally, sitting down next to Irene is Elena, a kind and warm woman. Elena volunteers on the El Paraíso Tourism Commission with Cristina. She lives in a large, beautiful home.

As is sometimes the case when we are seated with Hondurans, the topic of conversation shifts to life in the United States. Giovanni makes a seemingly innocent comment that sparks a fascinating conversation. "Life in the U.S. is difficult for immigrants," he says. I nod my head, grateful that he has acknowledged a fact that many in El Paraíso seem to overlook. "Yes," agreed Elena, "I don't know why anyone would want to go there." Irene puts her enchilada down and says that most people in El Paraíso have nothing. There is no work available, no hope of making money, so they leave hoping for something better in the U.S. "And," adds Giovanni, "there is opportunity for an education in the U.S. that does not exist here." Elena huffs, pulls her wool shawl tighter around her shoulders, and counters that in the U.S. only the very rich can afford to get a higher education. "Right, Kevin and Cristina?" I admit that costs to attend colleges and universities are becoming increasingly out of reach for many people but, of course, there are certainly infinitely better opportunities there than here. Giovanni sips his rice milk and nods, but Elena will have none of it.

"People are losing arms and legs trying to get to the U.S.," she says, noting a pattern that is reported in the Honduran newspapers and in at least one television documentary that a friend of mine saw referring to the horrific injuries suffered by Hondurans as they attempt to hop between trains bound for the U.S. "Who would risk death to go?" questions Elena, clearly not wanting an answer. Irene is restless in her seat and turns so that her entire body is facing Elena, irritated that her first response somehow vanished in the brisk January air. "They risk everything because they have nothing here. We are lucky because we have nice homes and jobs. The people who risk their lives are the very poor in search of a better life," she says, with a hint of frustration in her voice. Elena shakes her head in disagreement. "In the U.S., Hondurans will do any kind of work," Elena proclaims. "They do things they would never do here. They wash dishes!"

I nearly cough up my enchilada. Did I hear that right? If I hung a sign outside our front door tomorrow that read *Help Wanted. Person needed to hand wash my toilet with a toothbrush*, people would line up to take it. One day, while Cristina was out working, a young woman knocked on our door. With her six year-old son standing nervously behind, she asked to come in. While her son waited in the kitchen, she would be willing, for a small fee, to spend some time with me in the bedroom. It took a few minutes for me to unravel the request in Spanish, but when I did I was shocked. She moved sadly on to the next house. Compared to what some people do in El Paraíso to try to get by, washing dishes would be a dream job.

So, as I try to keep down my rice milk, Irene is squirming. Evidently annoyed to have to repeat herself, she looks at a spot on the table (maybe it will listen) and says softly, "Many people here have nothing. No future. Nothing." Elena doesn't want to hear a word and everyone seems to agree that it is best to end the conversation.

If Elena lived high on a mountain above El Paraíso, where the town looks so innocent and beautiful, I might understand her part in the conversation. But, the truth is, if Elena walked out her front door, turned left, and walked two blocks she would find several people who would tell her exactly why they would leave for the U.S. at that very minute, if given the chance.

A pastor in Boston I know once gave a sermon making a similar point. She used an analogy to explain that in the United States, many of us choose to build our homes with windows on only one side. We like the view of the sun setting over the ocean, the sounds of waves nestling onto the beach, and the feel of a cool ocean breeze. We don't put windows on the side of our house facing inland. It's easier to live life without facing that reality. Maybe this is the case with Elena.

No Big Deal

I'm sitting in a chair reading a book when our neighbors receive a phone call from an ophthalmologist in the U.S. who is in town as part of a church group. He and a group of friends from northern Minnesota make the trip once a year to help people in the poorer communities around El Paraíso. On this evening, the doctor calls wishing to speak to one of the two people who are supposed to go along with the group as translators the following morning. As it turns out, the two translators have bailed, and I am asked to replace them. Much to the amusement of my teenage neighbor, who knows firsthand my unique Spanish skills, I offer to go.

I meet the group, mostly middle-aged men, at the one small motel in town at 7 a.m. Some of the guys jump in a pickup truck and the rest of us pile into the back of an old truck that the doctor has rented from a man in town. We head for Las Vegas, a community about 30 minutes up the mountain beyond Cuyalí that, as far as I know, has no slot machines. Along the way we pick up the pastor of a local church and several others, including a young woman with two children, Rosa María. A few minutes into the ride, as we begin to climb the mountain, it becomes obvious the truck won't make it. Soon smoke is pouring out from under the hood, and the doctor is asking me to translate. I explain to the Hondurans that the truck is "broken" and that "some part is making smoke." We will leave this truck here and the other truck will take the rest of us up in groups. They nod, and I am excited that they have at least partly understood me.

As I savor my small victory, most of the Minnesotans gather around the engine of the smoking truck. From what I have gathered, the group consists of blue-collar workers who make a living working with their hands and enduring brutal winters. Suddenly, one of the guys looks up, points, and says, "What are they doing? Are they going to *walk*?" Sure enough, on the road up ahead, the women are walking, chattering away, and carrying the youngest children in their arms. Slightly ahead of them, running and laughing, are the other kids.

The broken-down truck is just a normal part of everyday life in El Paraíso. No big deal. We'll just walk. The Minnesotans, some visiting El Paraíso for the first time, nod and smile. Whether it's scraping up enough money for dinner, working a 10 – 12 hour day in the fields or a factory, or dealing with a broken-down truck, Paraiseños roll with the hand life has dealt them with a spirit that leaves foreigners shaking their heads in awe.

When a Bike Meets a Car

The main road leading into and out of El Paraíso is a cluttered mess. Buses, trucks, cars, bikes, horses, and pedestrians all share the street where traffic laws either do not exist or are not enforced. Cristina has been working hard with the local government in an attempt to bring some order to the mayhem. She is making progress, but like everything else, the process is slow. Rolling down the roads of El Paraíso are bikes carrying more than one person. I've seen as many as four children pile on: one on the handlebars, one on the bar, one steering and pedaling, and the other standing on the back. The danger of the situation is overshadowed by the awe of what the youngsters have accomplished. In a show of love, you will see a husband pedaling away while his wife rides on the handlebars.

Coming home from a visit with Janet, who is now helping me with some *charlas* at the high school, I stroll along the main road into El Paraíso. I hear something take a spill behind me. I turn back to see a young man picking himself and his bike up off the pavement. He seems okay, and I continue along the main highway back into town. Across the street, walking in the same direction, are two young women laughing and enjoying the beautiful afternoon weather. A minute later, the young man on the bike passes me and moves ahead. But something is strange. He can't seem to keep his bike in a straight line, and it is swerving dangerously. *Is he drunk?* He soon answers the question for me. Up ahead, a small red pickup truck is approaching. Suddenly, the man jerks his bike into the path of the oncoming truck. *Oh *!#*!* The truck swerves left; the bike swerves right and bang! The young man on the bike flips onto the hood, hits the windshield, and flops like a rag doll onto the road.

There is an eerie moment of silence before two men jump out of the passenger door of the truck. I begin running up to the scene, fearful at this point that the man is dead. My only thought is don't move him. As I arrive, the driver, clearly shaken, emerges from the truck. "What could I do? What could I do?" he says desperately, looking at me. I tell him it wasn't his fault and assure him he did nothing wrong. By now, the two men are holding the victim in a standing position and knocking the dirt off of him as if this will make everything better. "What do we do?" the driver asks me. *Not that!* is my first thought.

By some miracle, the victim does not look too bad. His face is badly bruised and I imagine he has several broken bones. He is conscious and the alcohol is most definitely masking the pain. "What do we do now?" the driver asks me again. I have no idea what the protocol is in El Paraíso. I imagine waiting for an ambulance is out of the question. Before I can come up with a good answer, the two friends of the driver lift the injured man up in a horizontal position by his arms and legs. Like a sandbag, they swing him back and forth, and on the count of three toss him into the back of the pickup truck. He lands with a bang and the two friends jump in the truck. The decision has been made to drive him to the hospital in Danlí.

When the alcohol wears off, the victim will have a very rude awakening. I hope that as he is recovering, someone explains to him just how lucky he is to be alive. Before the pickup truck came over the hill, several tractor trailers had raced past me. If it had been one of the tractor trailers, and not the pickup truck, there would have been nothing left of the young man to take to the hospital. Getting hit by the pickup truck was one of the better things that could have happened. That's something I never thought I'd say.

Blanquita

In preparation for another school year, I head over to Blanquita's house to go over a few ideas I have been tossing around since she asked me for help. Blanquita is the assistant director and in charge of the afternoon classes at María Garay, the school next to our house. The proximity of the school and her presence have motivated me to help her get things moving this year.

Blanquita is a rare flower in El Paraíso. She is the first educator I have met who believes that the function of a school extends beyond the classroom and the 12 – 5 schedule. She started a choir, a dance group, and the basketball team that I coached. We often practiced until 6 p.m. while Cristina played *UNO* with another group of students. When a few teachers complained about kids playing cards, Blanquita dismissed the petty complaints and encouraged kids to play. One student, who had been a discipline problem, became a model student when his behavior during the day determined whether or not he could play *UNO* with Cristina.

Blanquita stayed late and told me that she did so because kids in El Paraíso have no organized recreational outlets. Her dedication and open-mindedness is rare in the educational system of this town. So I shouldn't have been surprised about what would happen next.

I arrive at Blanquita's house, engage in a little small talk, but can't contain myself. I start spouting off all of the plans I have for us. Together, we are going to move education forward in El Paraíso. Her smile seems forced, and her usual happy demeanor is missing. "What is it?" I ask her. She tells me that she won't be back at María Garay this year. My heart sinks, and I feel my legs weaken a little as her words hit me in the gut. She can't do it anymore. She's tired. It seems that her radical ideas for making a school a place that develops the whole child have made some critics. The director of the school, an older woman who was Blanquita's teacher, did not see eye to eye with her former pupil.

It doesn't take a genius to figure out what was happening. In a town with an educational system content, even determined to stand in place, Blanquita is a threat. She leads by example, showing teachers that there is more to being an instructor than lecturing. She stayed late and spent hours outside of work finding ways to develop the kids entrusted to her care.

This year, Blanquita and I had plans to make better use of the small supply of school computers, make the school government an active body that did more than just get elected, add another basketball team, and provide teacher trainings outside of school hours. I felt like together we had a chance to do great things.

However, challenging the system, one as broken down as public education in El Paraíso, is a monumental battle for one person. Blanquita is a compassionate, soft-spoken woman whose soul was being trounced by those unable or unwilling to see her vision. So, as I stood in Blanquita's living room and felt the wind once again punched out of my sails, I felt sorry for the kids. For a brief time, while children in other schools were at the mercy of poor leadership and misguided agendas, kids in the afternoon session of María Garay were getting a glimpse into what a school could be: a place that cares about its kids and is led by a person who recognizes that each one is a gift.

Blanquita sees me sinking and apologizes. She can't keep up the fight. It's taking a toll on her physically. I had seen the signs at the end of last year. "We can still work together," she says, putting my feelings ahead of hers. "I know," I reply. "I just feel for the kids." She wants me to keep coming by the house for advice and to share my ideas. With her help, maybe we can make a difference in San Juan and Cuyalí. I need Blanquita much more than she needs me. I need her passion and her smile, and I need to know that in this town someone like her is around. I need to know that the fight isn't over and that from behind the scenes she can still be a voice of change for education. Otherwise, I fear she will fade silently into the background as I imagine so many other revolutionary thinkers have in El Paraíso.

Daniela

On the Pan American highway between El Paraíso and the Nicaraguan border sit three small bars. The places look innocent enough, a watering hole for lonely truck drivers in need of a beer.

It is what a number of women do behind the bar, in a row of tiny rooms, which grabbed my attention. The women are called Commercial Sex Workers (CSW), legal prostitutes who make their livings as sex objects to the men who frequent their place of business. According to the statistics, many CSWs were victims of some sort of sexual abuse or violence as children. Some have been in the business since they were as young as 13 years old. Approximately 20 percent of their clients are 15 – 19 years old, and 40 percent of their clients are married. Nearly all of the CSWs interviewed in a recent survey said that they were in the business of sex for one reason: survival. They have no choice. In El Paraíso, most of the CSWs have one or more children whom they are raising alone. Their work is dangerous, as they are often at the mercy of drunk and violent men. Needless to say, AIDS has ripped through the CSW community like wildfire. In San Pedro Sula, the industrial capital of Honduras, I heard it is estimated that over 15 percent of the CSWs have AIDS.

A few months ago, Erika asked me to assist in an AIDS *charla* being presented to CSWs working in the bars in El Paraíso. My part of the seminar was a question and answer session in the form of the game "Hot Potato" (played with a plastic ball). After the *charla*, a couple of the workers, headed by a young woman named Daniela, expressed interest in another seminar. When I asked the women what they would like to talk about, they said they didn't care. "As long as we get to play ball," they said. "Hot Potato" was a hit.

So I show up at the Health Center on a Thursday morning in February, the day when all of the CSWs are tested for sexually transmitted diseases. I suggest that we gather once a month to talk about health issues related to their work as well as other topics. We will begin on February 24. The response I receive is less than enthusiastic, with the exception of Daniela. "So," she exclaims, "On February 24 we play ball!"

About a week before our scheduled meeting, Erika suggests we visit the bars to examine the women's working conditions and possibly incorporate sanitation into the theme of our *charla*. On a hot afternoon we are walking to the bars when Daniela approaches from behind. "Hello!" she shouts, startling us a bit. I guess Daniela is in her late thirties, although she looks older than that. She is a short woman, of medium build, with short brown hair and bright eyes. Life as a CSW, a job she has been doing for 16 years, seems to have taken a toll on her body. She is, however, determined always to carry a smile.

We plan to visit Daniela's bar last, so she accompanies us to the first two. They are dark and dingy places, even on a bright sunny day. Daniela explains that the women who work here are probably sleeping, resting up to prepare for the long night ahead. So, checking out the conditions of the rooms is not an option.

Daniela leads us a little farther down the road to her bar. Like a proud tour guide, she takes us in and introduces us to the owner. A wiry, shirtless man with a crooked hat greets me with an awkward handshake. He blurts something that I don't understand and walks away, holding up his pants.

"That's an apple," Daniela says. "What's an apple?" I ask. "That," she says laughing and pointing to the wall. Adorning a large space is a painting of a naked woman kneeling on the beach. Between her legs, strategically placed, is, I suppose, an apple. I think it looks more like a pineapple, but figure it's not something worth debating.

While Erika is speaking to another worker, Daniela shows me her room. I walk into an eight-foot by eight-foot dwelling with no windows. Wires hang from the low ceiling, and a small waft of musty air seeps in through the gap between the wall and the ceiling. Daniela's bed is a six-inch thick twin mattress on a metal frame that sits about two feet off of the floor. She pushes aside a pair of leather pants, lifts the mattress, and shows me the rotting pieces of wood that keep her mattress from falling through the frame.

Daniela is now standing in front of a tiny night stand at the foot of the bed. "Now, Kevin, this is where I keep all of my things," she says pointing to her stand like a game-show hostess. "Look, I have all of my condoms here, my soap so that I can wash my hands when I'm done, toilet paper, deodorant, and my toothpaste." I'm a bit uncomfortable as I realize that Daniela is looking for my approval. "Everything looks good," I assure her. She smiles and says, "I know I'm poor, but I try to keep everything neat. You should see some of the other women's rooms. They have used condoms all over the floor." I think I'll pass on seeing those rooms, but at least they're using condoms.

As Daniela straightens her night stand, I begin to look around the room. Graffiti covers the walls and is missing only in places where the paint has chipped away. Daniela doesn't have a pillow, so she uses her bath towel. The blanket is dirty and her mattress appears to be developing mold. Beside her bed is a small bench where a few pairs of socks are drying. There is no air flow, and I am already feeling claustrophobic. I turn my head toward the door in a failed attempt to gasp some fresh air. In a few months, it will be much hotter, and I shake my head at the thought of her working and sleeping in such a place. Erika walks in, looks around, and says, "No window!"

Daniela sits down on the edge of her bed. "From here, I can see the bar," she says, looking out the door. "So, this is where I wait for the clients. When they enter the bar, I'll go out to get a beer and maybe dance a little."

Daniela makes 40 *Lempiras* ($2) per ten minutes that a man spends in her room. Most, she says, don't stay longer than ten minutes. Of the 40 *Lempiras*, she must pay ten to the owner to cover the cost of using the room. This is her rent, so to speak. Most of her clients come from El Paraíso. This week she has had only three clients. However, the week before she had 19. "It was a good week," she says. I imagine Erika, like me, is startled. Twelve CSWs times nineteen clients each in one week is a staggering number. I wonder how in the world AIDS has not yet crippled our little town.

I'm also wondering about Daniela's health. It is safe to guess that the 19 clients were not spread out evenly through the week, meaning it's likely she had as many as four or five in one night. "It's hard she says," looking at the ceiling. "If I'm having my period, or if I am sick or just sore, I'm required to work. If I choose to go to bed early, I must pay 50 *Lempiras* to the owner." It's rare that the owner ever makes 50 *Lempiras* off of a worker in one day, so the "fine" is outrageous from a strictly economic standpoint. Daniela looks at me and says, "Kevin, even if a woman is pregnant and not feeling well, she will still work." Now I am lightheaded: *pregnant women*! Daniela sees my reaction and explains that this is an awful place to work.

When Erika asks her if she has anywhere else to live if she chooses to leave, the gates open. Daniela has a daughter in town who refuses to let her live with her because of her work.

Daniela's eyes are tearing up as she looks at Erika. "If you told me right now that you had a job for me working in your house, I'd leave right now. You think I want to do this. I don't want this life." She grabs a tissue, wipes her eyes, and looks directly at me. "Kevin, I don't want this. I want to work in someone's house. I want to wash their clothes and clean for them. Sometimes, the woman in the restaurant down the street lets me wash dishes to make some money. I like that." She looks out the door and then back at me, trying to control her emotions. "I don't want this life. Every night I ask God to take care of me. I pray to Him," she says, clasping her hands and looking up at something far beyond the moldy ceiling of her cage. "I ask Him for help because I don't want this life!" She is shaking a little and looks like a frightened child who wants someone, anyone, to understand. I feel useless standing there, watching her sob and realizing I'm in over my head. Her life, her struggle is so far beyond anything I ever imagined. I say nothing.

She dries her eyes. I look away and let my eyes wander along the cracking, graffiti-covered walls and up to the ceiling. There is no light bulb, not even a space for one. At night, when she is working, the room is dark. I imagine this allows Daniela's mind to wander to a place far from this hell.

Daniela leads us out the front door of the bar and out to the main highway. "I'm going to get out of here Kevin," she says grabbing my hand to say goodbye. "But, I'm not leaving until after you give us your *charla*. I want to play ball!" she says, laughing. She gives my hand a squeeze, turns around and heads back to the bar. She will spend the night sitting on the end of her bed, staring out the door, hoping and dreading at the same time that someone will enter.

I return to our house and slump into a chair. For what seems like an hour, I sit and stare at the brilliant sunlight pouring into our front room. None of this is fair, and in this moment I am overwhelmed with sadness and guilt. I wonder about a God that allows such a world to exist, one with so much beauty yet so much suffering.

Cristina and I head to church this Tuesday evening. I need to hear the beautiful voices of the children's choir filling the empty space. Amidst their glorious music, I turn and look into the darkness of the night. Up the road a few miles, a trucker on his way to Nicaragua is making a stop. Daniela is dreaming of a far-away place when he walks in. I bow my head and ask God to take care of her.

So They Call This "Growth"

As we approach our one-year anniversary in Honduras and prepare for the beginning of a new school year, we reflect on how we are doing.

We arrived in El Paraíso full of energy, enthusiasm, and dreams. We were ready to serve and start making progress in a town anxiously awaiting our arrival. Well, there we were, and most days it seemed like nobody had told anyone we had arrived. Despite an initial general lack of interest from both the *Casa de la Cultura* and the Health Center (our assigned counterpart agencies), we continued knocking on their doors, reminding them we were here and weren't planning on going away. With a sporadic task here and there, our presence was largely ignored and our time and skills greatly underutilized by those who had asked for our help. Our excitement turned to disappointment. We didn't expect to walk into a parade, but we also didn't expect such indifference. We were here, after all, to help.

We began our work in the schools. While the kids greeted us with open arms, some teachers and the general craziness of the schools drove us insane. This, in combination with a lack of consistent work with our counterpart agencies, caused the disappointment to intensify. We found ourselves getting angry. On several nights we contemplated calling it quits. We missed our families, our friends, the U.S.A., and wondered why we were "wasting" our time banging our heads against a wall that wouldn't budge.

Then October rolled around and the wall moved a bit. A couple of small miracles in Cuyalí, meeting Blanquita, a successful end

126

to our work in the schools, and recognition that El Paraíso was growing on us made things start to look up.

Since returning from vacation in the U.S., we've noticed a change in ourselves. Setbacks, like the loss of Blanquita, are just another hurdle to overcome. Suddenly, both the local government and Health Center are seeking our help--not as much as we would like but more than before. Our persistence, at least for right now, has paid off.

The other day Cristina was invited by a couple of engineers to review a plan for a new community that will be built next to San Juan. She offered up her ideas, most of which were ignored. When she returned home that afternoon, we sat at our kitchen table and talked. "I think they listened to about ten percent of my ideas," Cristina said. We sat quietly, pondering this for a while. I smiled and looked up at her. "Not bad," I said. Cristina grinned and nodded: ten percent, a victory indeed.

We are learning a lot about life here. Walking down the street, we are greeted by good friends, young and old. Our Spanish is better, and we aren't the new gringos in town. We are part of El Paraíso. We are not special, but we are now neighbors which is more important. We have one year left here, but for everyone else this is the reality of their lives. Expecting the community to shift into fifth gear (or second for that matter) just because we are in town is, looking back, unfair and unrealistic. We are now trying to look at life through the eyes of our friends and coworkers.

When I came home with the sad news that Blanquita would no longer be at the school, Cristina said she was surprised at how well I was taking the news. Where anger once dominated such setbacks, something new now resides. Reality isn't always pretty, but it is liberating. We work with what we can. We learn to be disappointed for a moment and then plan how we will adjust. We are Paraiseños now, no more, no less. We live in a Third World town and this means nothing, absolutely nothing, is easy. It is selfish to think any other way. For the next year we will give our best, thankful for the opportunity.

Anger will resurface, but no longer will we let it knock us down. Get over it and move on. It is the only way.

A Difficult Decision

We originally planned to form leadership groups in San Juan, Cuyalí, and Monte Cristo. Now, instead, we have decided to form only two groups, making the difficult decision not to return to Monte Cristo. It is no secret that our experience in the school was negative. On three different days we walked 30 minutes to Monte Cristo only to find out school was canceled for the day. Despite leaving contact numbers, we were never notified about these cancellations. Our *charlas* seemed to inconvenience the fifth-grade teacher, and more often than not the director was not present. In short, we had no support.

Janet, who has been so helpful to us and is now a good friend, understands our decision. She is one of the most motivated people I've met here. I will continue to work with her in the high school.

Suddenly our time here seems short, and San Juan and Cuyalí offer an opportunity. Right now this seems like the correct thing to do. San Juan and Cuyalí are two of the poorest communities in El Paraíso and present the highest number of health problems among children. They also appear to lack any organized leadership. There is an opportunity to make a difference.

As for Monte Cristo, it is hard. We will miss the kids and may someday regret not giving it a shot. I have no idea if we have done the right thing.

Creating Leaders

In Cuyalí and San Juan, we will form two leadership groups, focusing our energy on select students who have shown the most potential. We have high expectations and hope for our sixth graders. Is it unfair to us and our kids to aim so high? We don't think so. We are no longer naïve, but we will not let our setbacks lower our expectations. By May, will our groups have dissolved, doomed by the realities of life in a poor community? Of course, this is possible, but time and again the kids have proven they are made of more than most adults realize. I'm betting on the kids.

Being a Kid

It's 6 p.m. and just about dark. There is a knock on our door. Standing outside is Fernando's mother; Fernando is a young boy who has taken a liking to us and often stops by our house to chat. She appears to be in a hurry. She walks into the house and explains that Fernando left the house at 8 a.m. to sell tortillas and has not returned. He has never been this late, and she is worried. We have not seen him all day. Cristina stays in the house in case he stops by, and Fernando's mother and I split up to cover different parts of town. I search frantically for over half an hour with no luck. I pass my friend Rafael's barber shop, and he stops me to say hi. Rafael is about my age and also the minister of a small evangelical church in San Juan. By coincidence, Fernando's mother attends the church, and Rafael promises to keep an eye out.

I return to the house and see Fernando's mom sitting alone on our front step. She comes inside the house, drinks some water, and we decide to walk up to San Juan to see if he has returned home. She seems rather calm and just hopes he has not gotten in a fight with some local kids who like to pester Fernando. Just as we leave the house, Fernando comes walking up. His mother clasps her hands in front of her face and shouts for joy. I'm happy but want to know where he's been. He has no good response. His mother is happy he is safe, so I don't persist.

The next evening, at 7:30, Fernando knocks on the door. Occasionally he makes a late run to sell tortillas, and tonight he is on his way back to San Juan. I can see something is bothering him. While he won't admit it, Fernando is scared to walk home alone at night. It seems that kids have been giving him a hard time, trying to lure him into a fight and even taking his money.

Stooped on our front doorstep under a peaceful El Paraíso sky, Fernando shares his situation. "I'm not afraid," he says. "They don't scare me." I nod my head and then offer to walk back with him. He doesn't hesitate. "Sure!" he says, sounding relieved.

While I have spent many days working in San Juan, I have never ventured up the hill at night. As we leave the scattered streetlights in town, I am amazed at how dark the road has become. After rounding the first curve, I cannot see more than ten feet in front of me. "That's where they wait," says Fernando, pointing at a row of trees that look eerie in the darkness. "They come out and form a circle around me, calling me names. I'm not afraid of them," he says, trying to convince himself more than me. "There is another group of kids in San Juan who have offered to teach me how to fight. My mom told me not to, but someday I may have to." As soon as Fernando mentions "group of kids" my first thought is gangs.

Fernando is an easy target. He lives with his mother and drug-addict brother. He is 11 years old, cannot read or write, and does not know the answer to 4 x 1. "Five," he said the other day when Cristina was working with him and a friend on multiplication tables. Fernando missed them all, started acting up to cover his embarrassment, and wound up knocking a glass off the table and shattering it. Last year he failed third grade because he never went to school. He's gang material, and I wonder how long he will stay on the straight path. I worry that one day he will get tired of being picked on and simply join his enemies. Let someone else get pestered for a change.

All of this is racing through my mind as we round another bend and approach the hill up to San Juan. Immediately before the ascent, there is a road off to the left, lit up by a streetlight. It is surreal watching people emerge from the darkness of San Juan, into the light, only to disappear again a second later.

As we pass through the light, Fernando grabs my arm and tells me to "watch out." Before I can say anything, I hear a high-pitched whizzzz and then, out of the darkness, only a few feet to my left, a bike flies past. I jump, and Fernando laughs. "Stay to the side or you will get hit," he says calmly. No need to tell me twice. I drop Fernando off in front of his house, and he says thanks. I give him a wave and head back down the hill, sure to stay far to the side.

When Does School Start?

As Cristina and I talk about the logistics of our leadership groups, in Cuyalí, we must find out if our kids will have classes in the morning or the afternoon. I have talked to teachers and read the newspaper; no one can agree on what day school will officially begin. A friend and teacher at one school told me that school will start on February 14. However, another friend and teacher told me classes will not begin until February 28. I just read in the paper that school is set to commence February 22. This is too much, so I decide to run my own independent survey.

In a friendly place like El Paraíso, this is an easy job. I just walk out the front door, say hello to friends and neighbors, and casually ask my survey question. In my very non-scientific study of roughly 20 people ranging in age from five to 60, I reached the following conclusion: Nobody has any idea. The following dates were given as a possible start date: February 14, 21, 22, 26 (a Saturday), 28, 30 (my favorite), March 1, and March 6. This is a mind-boggling scenario. In Cuyalí, the kids don't know if they have classes in the morning or afternoon. They have been out of school for over three months. We are picking up right where we left off last year. Not a good sign.

Rosa María

I hop off the bus and begin the familiar walk along the road to Cuyalí. A 30-minute walk from the main highway and fifteen minutes past the school lays the last house in this beautiful, but terribly poor community. It belongs to Rosa María, one of the women I met when the group from Minnesota was in town. She is a vibrant lady with a husband, two young children and a desire to learn the piano. For this reason, I am seeking her out. I have talked to Carlos at the *Casa de la Cultura* and found out they will be offering classes, so I want to confirm with her what times are best.

I know I am close to her house when I hear a young man shout, "Hola!" I am startled and turn to face him. Behind the man are two children and an older woman equally excited to see me. The woman, with a big smile on her face, says, "How is your mom?" I'm a bit confused, but people in Cuyalí are so friendly they may sincerely want to know how my mom is doing.
"She's fine," I reply.
"Oh that's great. When is she coming?"
"To Cuyalí?" I ask.
"Yes!"

I explain that I don't think my mom will be coming anytime soon. They are very disappointed, and I am both perplexed and flattered by their desire to meet my mother. The young man offers to walk me to Rosa María's house, and I am grateful. "Your mom is a wonderful person," he says, with a slur. "Oh, well, thank you. Yes, she is." This is getting weird. "We really enjoyed meeting her last time she came." Aha! This is a typical case of confusing the gringos. We both have a good laugh as I explain to him that he has confused me with someone else. It seems the woman he is talking about was part of a medical brigade that passed through months ago, and I look like her son.

"That's it," he says pointing to a small house set back off the road. I can see Rosa María sweeping her front step and Daniel, her five year-old son, running out to greet me.

I shake the man's hand and tell him I'll be sure to tell my mother he says hi. He doesn't get my joke, but he laughs anyway.

"Keveen!" shouts Daniel as he opens the barbed wire fence to let me in. Rosa María waves me into the house to an empty plastic chair, and I have a seat. Ana, her three-year-old daughter, gives me a big hug, and I can see that both she and Daniel are covered in dirt. "Three days without water," says Rosa María, obviously flustered. "We can't shower or clean the dishes, and my plants are dying." Sure enough, the beautiful gardens that Rosa María has filled with a variety of plants and trees look barren. I can't remember the last time it rained, and the cracking soil beneath the trees is proof that it's been awhile. The wells in Cuyalí are dry, and it is miles to the nearest water source, so the family is conserving every drop.

She pulls up a chair, and we start talking. When I first met Rosa María, I wrongly assumed that she must be one of the rare people with a little money in Cuyalí. Her young, bright face, full set of white teeth, and clear Spanish led me to what I now realize was a wrong conclusion. In simple terms, Rosa María and her family are poor--very poor. Her husband spends his days working a farm and earning 40 *Lempiras* ($2) a day, barely enough to get by.

Their house is dark and musty, and the only furniture is a small wooden table and a few plastic chairs. Curtains blow in the wind, separating the four rooms of the house. In the "kitchen" is a refrigerator, unplugged (it appears she uses it only for storage), and a two-burner stovetop that looks like it's on its last legs. The kitchen has one window, permanently closed to prevent the dust from getting in the food. Back in the living room, I watch from my chair as dogs, chickens, and ducks run in and are chased out by Rosa María and her broom. I practically leap out of my seat as a chicken comes scurrying out from behind a curtain, squawking and running as if death itself is on its heels. The life of a chicken is stressful, and I do not envy these creatures.

Inevitably, a chicken or duck leaves behind some droppings on the concrete floors of the house. Daniel has disappeared in search of oranges, but Ana is running back and forth from the kitchen to the front yard. "Be careful!" I yell each time she comes by, but more times than not she runs barefoot through the droppings. She shows me her coloring book, but all I see are black fingers and fingernails and dirt caked to her pretty little face. She points to a picture, smiles, and runs out the door.

Rosa María comes out of the kitchen to join me. "Oh, Kevin, life without water is difficult." Difficult? That's the understatement of the century. How about impossible! Rosa María smiles and asks me about my family. I find out she has been married for seven years. She gave birth to Ana in the room adjacent to where we are sitting. "No one would let us borrow their car, and we couldn't get in touch with the Health Center. So I had Ana right there. I thought I was going to die." There is no health center in Cuyalí. While many communities without centers have volunteers trained in health, I have found no one in Cuyalí with such skills. If Rosa María or one of her children is sick, they must walk 45 minutes to the main road, ride the bus to El Paraíso, and then walk another 10 minutes to the Health Center. The cost is 12 *Lempiras* round trip, 24 if her husband or one of the children goes. That is half of a day's salary.

Daniel comes bounding through the front door, plows through the duck droppings, and presents me with a bag of oranges from their tree. "For orange juice!" he exclaims. "Now, let's play." Rosa María is off to make lunch (I feel guilty staying for lunch but know it would be more offensive to leave), so I am on Daniel duty. He rolls out this gigantic red thing that I now realize is a ball that needs to be blown up.

"Here!" he says, handing me a small plastic hand pump. He watches earnestly as I pump my arm. I switch from right to left, as my arms are losing the battle against this ball that was no doubt left by a gringo who probably never had to pump it up. I curse this unknown person as Daniel watches, evidently disappointed at how long it's taking me. "Are you sure you're pumping right?" With beads of sweat pouring down my forehead, I assure Daniel that I have things under control.

Ten minutes and a hernia later, we are outside playing. The ball, at full size, is larger than Ana, who is not sure if the ball is a toy or something that is going to eat her. Daniel is having a blast, kicking and chasing it around the yard. Okay, he's kicking, and I'm chasing. Then, all hell breaks loose.

Somehow the family bull has worked his way through the barbed wire gate and is in the forbidden territory of the front yard. The donkey is right behind. Rosa María's dogs, three of them, begin barking loudly and nipping at the heels of the bull, who is using his horns to fend off the attackers. This is enough for the donkey, who quietly exits the way he came in. But the bull is determined to stay, and Daniel springs into action. Armed with a long stick, he begins whacking the bull in an attempt to redirect him out the gate. I step aside as the bull runs around the right side of the house and nearly tramples the now wide-awake pig that was enjoying a late morning nap. I am laughing hysterically until, in a terrifying turn of events, Daniel decides to redirect the bull . . . towards me. Holding the oversized ball in my arms, I leap from the dirt to the safe haven of the back porch. Ana, standing a few feet to my left, evidently anticipating Daniel's bizarre skills at driving a bull, nearly falls over giggling.

The bull is now safely outside the fence and life returns to normal. Daniel and I are playing ball while Ana is carving a stick with a small, blunt machete. She drops her pants and takes a pee, pulls up her pants, and continues playing with the stick. She is sitting in her pee when I walk over and tell her that playing in and around her pee can make her very sick and that she should use the latrine next time. She smiles, picks up the machete, and moves to another spot.

Now lunch is ready. I have a seat with Daniel on a plastic stool at a small wooden table. Lunch is a plate of spaghetti and tortillas. "I'm so sorry Kevin. Without more water I can't make anything else." I imagine that feeding me is a sacrifice for Rosa María and her family, and I assure her that the food is perfect.

After a year in Honduras I have become somewhat desensitized to certain aspects of poverty. However, as I notice during lunch, there is much that still twists my insides and makes me nauseous. The sheer number of flies around the food is disturbing, and one lands in my spaghetti and drowns itself in the sauce. A duck poops by my foot, and the smell lingers as I am now forcing down the food. Flies swarm around Daniel and his filthy hair, as he sucks down a cup of Coca-Cola. The musty, dark room, the smell of animal feces, the buzzing of the flies, and the vision of Ana playing in her own urine make me lightheaded, and I am barely able to finish my lunch. I move outside immediately for some fresh air.

Good news. The neighbor's *pila* has some water, and they've offered to let Daniel and Ana use it to bathe. Rosa María and I sit in the house and continue talking. "For economic reasons, I never had a chance to continue my studies after high school," she says, looking thoughtfully out the front door and into her dying garden. "Now, I want to learn something new, like how to play the piano." She would like to have classes one morning a week, and I tell her I will be back in two weeks with more information.

Daniel and Ana join us, in clean clothes and looking refreshed. Daniel offers to accompany me to the corner of the dirt road as Rosa María hands me the plastic bag filled with oranges. They escort me to the front gate, and Rosa María gives me a big smile and waves goodbye. She scoops up Ana and walks slowly back to her house. Along the way, she leans over one of her plants and holds the wilting flower in her hand. Above her the unrelenting sun beats down, and Ana squints. No rain is in sight.

I say goodbye to Daniel and tell him I will return in soon. His job is to make sure the ball doesn't deflate and, for heaven's sake, figure out a way to keep the bull out of the front yard. He laughs and heads home.

A few minutes into my return voyage to the main road, I kick something. I look down and notice that several oranges have slipped out of a growing hole in my plastic bag. On hands and knees I attempt to corral the oranges back into the bag. Then, to my dismay, the bag rips in two pieces. I stuff some oranges in my pockets and attempt to carry the rest in the remainder of the bag. Up ahead, a young, barefoot girl is running towards me, waving something in the air. She says nothing as she approaches. With a smile and an outstretched hand, she presents me with a plastic bag. Then, she turns and runs back to her house where I see her mother smiling and waving. "Gracias!" I yell. She smiles and returns to sweeping her front porch. With a bag full of oranges, I am on my way.

Clear Water Is Not Clean Water

In a small community just up the mountain from El Paraíso, a young child, less than two years old, has died. María, the nurse in charge of the diarrhea prevention program at the Health Center, has asked me to go along to investigate the cause and talk to community members about prevention. Accompanying us is Javier, another Health Center worker. A middle-aged man with a matter-of-fact attitude, Javier is one of the most knowledgeable individuals I've met when it comes to understanding health conditions in Honduras.

Together, the three of us make the 45-minute walk to the first of the houses we want to visit. Our last stop will be with the parents of the child who died. We move from house to house, mostly cases of extreme poverty, and give advice. Javier is thorough, checking the latrines and asking questions about how the families prepare their water and food. He has seen all this before, but even he didn't seem prepared for what we encounter in the next house.

As we walk through a small front gate and up a narrow path to the house, I begin to hear a low buzzing sound. It grows louder as we near the house, and suddenly María, Javier, and I are frantically swatting the air in front of us. There are flies and if someone told me there were 10,000, I would believe them. Sitting on the front porch, watching three strangers do an odd dance, is a mother with three young children between five and 12, and a young mother (a neighbor) with a nine-month old on her lap.

"What is going on with the flies?" blurts Javier before we have a chance to introduce ourselves. He, like me, wants to get to the point.

The mother throws up her arms as if to say, "You're telling me!" Javier quickly discovers the culprit. Beside the house is a two-foot high pile of coffee bean pulp with a circumference of at least six feet. Like many others, the woman, her husband, and children are living beside a small coffee farm, charged with the job of maintaining and guarding it from thieves. The owner of the farm, who lives in the city of El Paraíso, dumped the pile beside the house, planning to use it as natural fertilizer. This is a good gesture for the environment, but his choice of location is absurd. The woman explains that the flies are into everything, and they are helpless to stop them.

Standing on the front porch I can see the flies moving around in the house, swarming the food cooking on the *fogón*, and circling the small children. I continue swatting furiously in front of my face when Javier tells me to follow him to the well where the family draws its drinking water. Behind the house, we locate a couple of rotting boards that half-cover the opening of the well. Javier and I peer inside. Several leaves sit on top of murky water. "I hope they're not drinking this stuff straight," he says.

Back at the house, Javier is shaking his head in disbelief as the mother tells him the water in the well is clean. "The owner told us the water is drinkable." Javier explains that clear water doesn't mean clean water and shows the woman how to treat it with chlorine.

Meanwhile, María talks to the young mother. María wants to find out if her baby has been vaccinated. "Yes," says the mother. "Do you want me to show you her vaccination card?" María says yes. The young mother smiles, sets her baby, naked from the waist down, on the ground, and walks next door. Javier, who has already filled up a page in his notebook with sanitary problems in this house, looks ready to rip his hair out. "She—she--do you see this?" he yelps pointing at the baby. The child, nearly lost in a swarm of flies, runs his hand along the ground and then shoves his fingers in his mouth. It appears he hasn't been bathed in weeks. His nose is running and a streak of dirt is caked between his nose and upper lip. María just nods sadly as the child sucks on his dirty fingers.

The young mother returns with the vaccination card, and María talks to her about the dangers her son currently faces. In Honduras, diarrhea kills.

Another young child, maybe 12, with matted hair and filthy clothes, emerges from the house coughing uncontrollably. Her face is red, her eyes are watering, and she is gasping for breath in between hacks. Finally, she catches a breath and sits down slowly on the bench, moving more like an 80-year-old woman than a child. Every few minutes she starts hacking again, and Javier urges the mother to bring her to the Health Center. Good advice, but will it be taken?

In the past 15 minutes, this woman was told she needed to move the pile of coffee pulp, buy chlorine for her water, buy a small dropper for adding the chlorine, clean up her kids, cover her latrine, and get her daughter to the Health Center in town. She is living in a fly-infested home and trying to raise three kids on virtually no money. I wonder what she is feeling right now. Whatever it is, she doesn't reveal anything and waves as we plow through the flies on our way to the main road. "Kevin," Javier asks, looking over at me, "Have you ever seen anything like that before?" I'm a bit shaken and simply shake my head. Javier nods. Neither had he.

By the time we arrive at the home where the young child died, we are exhausted. I learn from Javier that the mother has given birth to nine children. Four of them were lost in one way or another to diarrhea.

Her husband is sitting on the front porch when we arrive, and he greets us as we sit down. The mother, 36-years-old but looking like she is in her fifties, doesn't speak. "How does your family drink the water?" Javier asks. The father adjusts his worn baseball cap and points out to the yard where a black hose carries water from the mountain and into a bucket. "That water is clean. Look how clear it is. We drink it just like that," he says proudly.

By now, he is flanked by three young children who smile at us uncomfortably. The mother is standing quietly in the doorway, a few yards behind her husband, with her arms folded over her chest. Javier explains that clear water doesn't mean clean water. "Oh, of course," belts the father. "We always use chlorine. That water is dirty." We all know he is lying, and Javier is obviously annoyed. Every recommendation Javier offers, the father has an "of course" response. We spend a very short time at the house, aware that we are making no progress. It's time to go home.

On the long walk back to town, Javier talks about the ignorance of many in El Paraíso and their unwillingness to change, even in the face of death. I am shocked that a woman who has lost four children to a preventable illness appeared so indifferent. However, I imagine she is not. I cannot think of a reason why she and her husband don't treat their water. Maybe they don't like the taste, an excuse I've heard used by people in San Juan. Maybe it's the notion that it really doesn't matter what you do. When you're very poor, losing a child is part of life.

"The children, Kevin. They are the hope of Honduras," says Javier as we descend the mountain. "Get your leadership groups formed and teach them. Maybe they will be willing to change." "Okay," I say softly.

Our rowdy group of youngsters, with so many challenges and obstacles in their paths, are the hope of this country? I know he's right. Javier is walking several steps ahead of me now, gazing down the mountain into the city of El Paraíso. María is at his side, sucking on a piece of sugarcane, possibly wondering if our four hours up here did any good. No matter. The fights here in El Paraíso are not won in hours. They are barriers you chip away day by day. For now, the sugarcane is sweet, and the sun is shining brightly. Tomorrow, we try again.

More of the Same

"The mayor has spent four years in office, and obviously no one told him he was mayor."
- A frustrated citizen of El Paraíso

It is a stifling hot day. I am lying in the hammock on our back porch, enjoying a good book, and trying to move as little as possible. Then I hear Cristina come in the front door. She marches swiftly through the kitchen and the screen door to the patio flies open. This cannot be good news. I put down my book and look into her moping eyes. "This has not been a good day," she says.

Next to San Juan, an international non-profit group has designed a new community to be built next year. A copy of the plan was given to the El Paraíso municipal government to review and make suggestions. Cristina and the engineers were impressed that they were asked for input and made several suggestions for improving the community. Their ideas took into account the future growth and changes that were likely to occur. When the project was presented, the project architect became defensive. She did not want to make any changes and threatened to move the project to another town.

The proposed community, House of Gold, calls for the construction of 55 new homes and will have its own water and sewage system. These are two very nice luxuries that the neighbors in San Juan can only dream of. It is a potentially wonderful project, but Cristina and the engineers felt it needed a few adjustments.

Today Cristina has learned that the mayor and councilmen have approved the project as originally planned. Antonio, who shared the reasoning behind the proposed changes in the final meeting, gave Cristina the bad news. "Aren't you mad?" asked Cristina. "I could be," he said, "but what is the point? They do whatever they want."

Perhaps the mayor and councilmen caved to the architect who was threatening that the group could pull the project, but it is more likely that in the end they just didn't care. What did it really matter if this new community was well-prepared for the future, or even the present? Some group with money was offering to build a community. Just let them build it. In the meeting, Antonio went on record and made it clear that if and when problems arise the engineers are not responsible. The problem, it seems, is that no one is ever responsible. In El Paraíso, you waste a lot of time cleaning up the mess someone else created.

So Cristina, an engineer and city planner, is upset. She was excited to be involved in such a potentially positive project, only to have her ideas and experience ignored. We try to understand why this always seems to happen in El Paraíso: why things don't ever seem to be well-thought-out, but quickly realize the pointlessness of our endeavor. I make room for Cristina in the hammock. She lies down and looks up at the sky. "Do you want beans for dinner?" she asks. Time to move on.

Why Not San Juan?

I didn't really realize how much I cared about San Juan until I heard about House of Gold going up right next door. I wonder how it will impact the community. The poor of San Juan, with their aging, weakly constructed homes, dirty water, and lack of a sewage removal system, are now watching a brand new planned community pop up. The people moving in had to meet certain financial requirements that most, if not all, in San Juan can't begin to touch. What are the people of San Juan thinking? Will it be yet another reminder of their poverty? Will they wonder why this group didn't use the money to improve their eroding community? Will they watch with sadness as the bulldozers topple their beautiful trees, a source of pride as well as shade on these brutal sunny days?

If I know the people of San Juan, most of them will not give it a second thought. At least, on the surface, they won't really care. However, on the inside, where their pride and self-esteem dwells, I hope this is not another blow to their spirit.

Gringo Alert

Cristina and I are sitting in *Café D'Palo* with Nagisa awaiting the arrival of two friends. We are laughing about something that happened earlier that day when a man, about 40 and with some graying hair, approaches our table. "Can I say hi?" he says in English, obviously recognizing fellow gringos in the room. Nagisa, who speaks a little English (we communicate with her in Spanish) says hello. He asks what Cristina and I are doing in Honduras but doesn't really seem interested. Before we can complete a sentence, he interjects, "Yeah, I'm a volunteer, too. I'm here for a week during my vacation helping out at the hospital in Danlí," he says, grabbing his belt. We are happy to hear this news and tell him so. He asks us where we are from and then, without hesitation, says, "I'm from Manhattan. I live right downtown. This is my first trip to Honduras," he explains, turning to face a young Honduran woman waiting patiently by the door and looking very bored.

"I met her (pointing his nose to the door) at the internet place here, and I thought she looked good, so I started talking to her," he says proudly. "And, here we are. You know, it will make my friends back home jealous," he says with a laugh, and a "right buddy" look at me. I smile politely and look at Cristina who is probably ready to knee this man in the very anatomy he plans to use later on. "Are you two married?" he asks, pointing back and forth at Cristina and me. We say yes, and he says, with a grunt, "Yeah, I've been down that road a few times." He looks over his shoulder to the young lady, turns back and says, "I better go, she's waiting." We shake hands, and he heads off.

Out of sight and out of mind, we enjoy a nice evening of music with our friends.

However, back at home, the man from the bar, whom we refer to as "Manhattan," is on our minds. The more we talk, the more disgusted we both get. It's those moments, when I'm face to face with someone like Manhattan, that I don't like myself. I was polite, smiled, shook his hand, and let him walk out the door to screw that young woman without even a word of protest.

So here is a note to anyone, future Peace Corps Volunteer, doctor, aide worker, vacationer, etc.: If you're coming down to Honduras because you can't get laid at home, and think it might be nice to take advantage of a young woman down here, STAY HOME! It is unbelievable how destructive such behavior can be. It diminishes the work of every American who works in Honduras. It is possible, with little effort sometimes, for a gringo to have sex with a Honduran woman if she thinks for one second it is her ticket out of town. And no doubt there are sex-starved men out there willing to take advantage of this unfortunate reality.

Manhattan will return to the U.S. and tell his family about the wonderful work he did and the sacrifices he made to help the people of Honduras. Then, he will head to the bar, whip out his camera, and show all his buddies a picture of the *senorita* he banged in El Paraíso. They'll all have a good laugh and order another round of beers.

I'm ill thinking that such people are running around representing the people of the United States. I should have told him that, but I didn't. That is my fault, and in a way I feel I let down the beautiful people of El Paraíso. I hope next time I will represent myself, my wife, my country, and Honduras better.

Breathing Exercises Are Good

It is Thursday afternoon, three weeks into the school year, and I am off to Cuyalí. I plan to meet with the sixth-grade teacher, explain the leadership groups we will be starting, and get her input. It is strangely quiet as I enter the gate to the school. Then I realize there are no kids. Classes have apparently been canceled. I stick my head in a classroom where a meeting is taking place among all of the teachers. "Come in Kevin, have a seat," says a teacher I recognize. For the next 20 minutes I listen to the group discuss plans for how they will celebrate Father's Day and who will participate in the parade on the anniversary of El Paraíso which is approaching.

The familiar fire is burning in my stomach as I now see the reason for canceling classes is to plan a party! I do my breathing exercises and wait patiently to talk with the sixth-grade teacher (also the director of the school), who is leading the meeting. During a break she stands up, offers me a few minutes of her time, and I scurry after her like a puppy. I rush through the information, and had I been explaining to her a root canal procedure, she could not have looked more excited. Every part of her body language, from her shifty eyes, to the rustling of her papers, to the tapping of her foot, says, "Get on with it!" When I show her the list of kids I've picked for the leadership group, and ask for her input, she refuses to look at it. She is sure my list is fine. Breathe, breathe . . .

I politely pack up my bag, thank her for her time, and wander back out onto the road, unusually calm and content. This year is about the kids, and the more time I spend in the school, the more excited I am to get started. I have no idea if our leadership groups will come together, but I know these kids deserve the chance to show what they can do.

"Hola Keveen!" shouts a woman resting comfortably with another woman, under a tree and out of the sun. I greet them, and recognize that one of the women is a parent of one of the kids I taught last year. "How is the girl?" she asks. I tell her Cristina is doing fine. "Are you two relaxing?" I ask. "Oh yes, we're waiting for a ride. We wouldn't think of walking to the bus stop in this heat!" she says with a laugh. I tell her I'm going to keep walking. "You're young and crazy," the older woman next to her says, and they both start laughing and waving good-bye. I smile and continue along. You can't help but love this place.

Reading in El Paraíso

Cristina and I walk next door to talk with the second-grade teacher at María Garay school where we will be working with five of her students who cannot read. While there, we also stop by the library that each class visits twice a week for 45 minutes. We walk in and see the librarian working with a third-grade class on a word search. We look around and after about two minutes we make the sad discovery that not a single book in the library is suitable for beginning readers. This explains why the kids are doing a word search.

What happened? How is it that a country can be so poor, so lacking in nearly every imaginable educational resource? How come we have so much at home and they so little? I'm beside myself with the realization that the school library has no children's books. How is anyone in this country learning to read?

The library at the *Casa de la Cultura* has a few children's books and no books for teenagers and young adults. It is mostly filled with old, donated books that never come off the shelf. As one teacher in El Paraíso said, "Those books are there so we have something to occupy the bookshelf. They are never read."

Reading, in any other form other than copying text from a book for homework, is not a part of the culture here. When a package of new books arrived from Tegucigalpa, including several good children's books, the box sat on the floor in an office until Cristina and I found it and put the books out on display. Reading for fun does not happen. Very few kids or adults who can read ever pick up a book for leisure. Parents don't read to their kids and, due to the lack of resources, neither do the teachers. What can we do to change this?

Poverty is such an awful beast. The things that just about every kid and adult in the U.S. take for granted, libraries stacked and overflowing with every book on every subject imaginable, is like an endangered species here: You see it only in pictures.

New Furniture

"Cristina! Cristina!" The shouts continue flying over our back wall until Cristina opens the back door and presents herself. It's about 8 a.m. and our neighbor Lourdes, still wearing her nightgown, tells Cristina she has an old couch that she no longer uses. Would we like it? Yes! We are both tired of sitting on plastic chairs all day long and my aching butt is proof. "Okay!" she says. "I'll bring it over!"

We are excited and skeptical. A few weeks ago, Lourdes' mother, Doña Romany, offered us a table that the family did not use. We were short on workspace, so Cristina and I decided to check it out. Doña Romany led us to the door of a room on the side of her house. She tried unsuccessfully to unlock the door, and Cristina took over. Turning the key and lowering her shoulder into the door, it flung open. Dust poured out through the door and showered us immediately. My white T-shirt turned brown. Cristina and I coughed and waved our hands frantically as we entered the room. Doña Romany showed no signs of being bothered and marched in like a general entering a building her troops had just secured. "It's a little dusty in here," she says. She points to an old table, or what may have at one time been a table, and announces, "This is it. Do you want it?" She answered her own question with a quick "No."

Doña Romany has a funny habit of expecting the worst. She always answers her own questions with an abrupt "No." On many occasions, she has passed freshly made and absolutely delicious food over our back wall. Each time we return the empty plate to her, she says, "Did you like the food . . . No." I always try to slip in "yes" before she can say "no" but have had no luck thus far. When we tell her the food was wonderful, she smiles, clasps her hands together in front of her face, and beams. It makes you feel good to see her so happy.

However, there is a big difference between a hot tamale, filled with meat, potatoes, and vegetables, and the piece of "furniture" being offered to us. The top of the table had four or five large, deep holes. If Doña Romany were to lean on the table, or simply put her pencil down, it might well collapse. The thickness of the dust covering the top indicated the table had not moved in several years. We did not, under any circumstances, want that thing.

We said nothing, but it was okay. Even Doña Romany seemed surprised by the condition of the table. "Yeah," she said looking disgustedly at the table, "you don't want it." We told her we were very grateful for the offer but that we just need something with a smoother surface to work on.

About a week later, early in the morning, Cristina and I heard someone or something banging around on our back porch. I looked out the back door and told Cristina to come see this. Being passed over our back wall from one man to another was a rather large, very nice looking table. It was just what we needed, and I peeked over the wall to thank Doña Romany who I imagined was probably overseeing the transfer. When she saw my face, she smiled. "This one is better, right?" she said, already knowing the answer.

So we now await, with anticipation and a little fear, the arrival of our new couch. There is a knock at the front door, and Lourdes and her son enter. To our delight, a short, wood-framed couch with small cushions is set down in our front room. After one year in plastic chairs, we are thrilled and thank Lourdes several times. To show our appreciation, we send them home with some fresh watermelon we have just cut.

As they leave, Cristina and I plop down on our "new" couch. The wood is rather old, the cushions faded, and the couch was certainly built for someone much smaller than I. We can't help but laugh. Two years ago, in the comfort of our Atlanta apartment, we never would have touched this couch. We might even have labeled it as "junk." We would not have appreciated such simple beauty. Now it is by far the most elegant thing in our home, and we bounce around on the cushions, laugh, and enjoy every moment of this glorious new piece of furniture.

"Cristina! Cristina!" It is Lourdes again, setting a bowl on our back wall. It is, of course, not empty. In place of the watermelon we had given her, is a large piece of honeycomb, dripping with fresh, all-natural honey. Lourdes tells us to break off pieces, suck out the honey, and spit out the honeycomb when we're finished. I walk inside the house, laughing. The generosity of the people of El Paraíso is heartening. Cristina joins me at the table as we prepare to dig in. Any doubt about the freshness of the honey is answered immediately, as a dead bee slides out of the honeycomb into the bowl. Not a bad way to die, I think, dropping a honey-drenched piece of honeycomb into my mouth.

A year ago, I can safely say, we would never have eaten anything that had recently expelled a dead and rather large insect. But things have changed. We rip off the honeycomb piece by piece. As our teeth sink in, the flavor of the honey explodes in our mouths. We chew away, big smiles on our faces, honey running down our cheeks. After sucking every last bit of honey, we spit out the honeycomb and dive back in.

It is a wonderful morning, a tribute to the people of El Paraíso. They have taught us the joy of giving, the pleasures that can be found in things we overlook every day, and we both recognize we have changed for the better, having lived in this town. I think I'll go take a nap on my new couch.

In *Their* Time

Some days I spend most of my time feeling as if I'm running in place, frustrated with the people with whom I'm supposed to be working and wondering if anything I am doing is making or will make any difference. Other days, I enjoy a nice walk around this precious town, absorb the beauty of the surrounding mountains, talk to the many friends I've made, and bask in the spirit and generosity of the people who call this place home. Then there are those rare days, ones that I've come to truly cherish, when some outside, mystical force seems to enter my mind, and I am able to see things more clearly. Emotions and challenges that yesterday could not be explored, suddenly, like a puzzle I can't solve, that I must walk away from and return to, become much clearer.

We have taken on many projects in the past year, some that crashed before getting off the runway, others that looked promising but never transpired, and finally those that seem to be moving forward. We have learned over the last year to accept that what we would like for El Paraíso is not necessarily what the community is ready for or wants, at least right now.

A dream of ours is to create a children's and young adult's section with new books within the public library at the *Casa de la Cultura*. The problem of illiteracy is not going away and won't begin to be solved until a culture of reading is created.

We dream of a glorious new section of the library for children and teens where they will feel comfortable and excited searching for a book to read. We want to see the *Casa de la Cultura* incorporate fun reading activities into their daily or weekly events. We've discussed these ideas with staff at the *Casa de la Cultura* with little success. Right now, El Paraíso is simply not ready. A lack of good books and a general apathy among the people of our town when it comes to the importance of reading have combined to form a difficult obstacle to overcome.

Creating a culture of reading is a long-term process, something we certainly cannot do in our short time here. Just because people in our community are not ready right now does not mean they will never be ready. If we can help increase the number of quality children's books and get a few more young people excited about reading, then, with the help of others, we will have done something important.

Fortunately, we have many friends at home itching to get involved in our work here. A plan is in the works to call upon them to help this dream of ours become a reality.

Pow Wow

These leadership groups are driving me batty! I just visited Cuyalí, had another bad experience with the school, and now I am questioning my thinking. This seems to happen roughly every 20 minutes. I planned to choose 12 kids from the 26 that I taught a year ago (there were actually 31 but five either failed or dropped out of school). When I'm confused and need some good advice, there is one person I can always turn to. Cristina pulls out the bag of Hershey's chocolates, a gift from home. We sit down at the kitchen table and get down to business. For over an hour, we share ideas, debate, develop ideas, throw them out, start over again, and finally reach a conclusion. It is the beauty of marrying the right person, always having your best friend nearby.

By the time we finish, we both feel like we have run a marathon. We slump farther down in our chairs, sip our water, and congratulate ourselves on what looks like a good plan but what will most likely get tinkered with several more times.

We simply cannot select 12 kids from a group that was, for the most part, dedicated. Plus, we have the support of their parents, and this is crucial. This year Cristina will join me in Cuyalí, so we will give the opportunity to all 26 kids. In order to make this work, we need to dedicate more time to Cuyalí. We will teach the course once a week for 90 minutes and spend the rest of the morning visiting the families of the kids.

In San Juan, we select 16 kids and will do the same thing. If these groups are to succeed, I feel we must do everything possible to give them the chance. By taking the time to meet their parents, see their homes, and spend some time with their families, maybe more kids will stick with us.

The groups are voluntary and will meet outside of school hours. Based on what we've heard from other Peace Corps Volunteers, we feel that if, after three months, we have four to six dedicated kids in each community, we will have something to be proud of. Here goes nothing!

Selection Day - San Juan

The big red door to the San Juan school stares us down. We are here to speak with the eight boys and eight girls we have selected for the leadership group. It is a big moment. All of the work we did last year and all of the planning we have done the past few months have brought us to this day when our venture begins.

The sixth-grade teacher sees us, welcomes us with a big smile, and waves us into the classroom. Cristina and I explain to the class that we have chosen 16 kids but that everyone in this room is important to us. We would love to have all of them but simply can't. It is not an easy moment for us, but the kids are smiling and seem to understand. As the teacher reads the names, I step outside to direct them under a few large trees where we will meet. One by one they emerge from the classroom. They are very excited, and that is a good sign. Even more important is that they respect their fellow classmates by heeding my advice not to show too much emotion. They exit the room, scurry across the basketball court, and begin to form a circle.

They watch with anticipation and let out a small yelp of excitement as each new member joins the group. There is silence as it appears that all members are present. But wait! There is a gasp, looks of confusion and some giggling as the final member makes his triumphant appearance. Arms extended outward and moving his body like an airplane, Denis flies across the court and into the group. Most members tower over him, but he does not care. I imagine no one was more surprised that he got selected than Denis.

The group is an interesting assortment of characters. There are several girls, outgoing and confident who succeed in the classroom with ease. However, there are also quiet kids who are easily lost in a class of 40 but who we notice have potential. There is Karen, who we affectionately call "too cool for school" because she makes a point to appear thoroughly miserable all the time. On the rare occasion you catch her smiling, she wipes it off her face immediately. No, she is not having fun.

Then, there is Denis, a little kid with a big personality. He goofs off a lot, rarely looks like he is paying attention, but has a characteristic that is absent in nearly all the kids we work with: He is a creative thinker. He reads into things, looks beyond the obvious, and often gives insightful answers just when you thought he had no idea what was going on. We look around the circle remembering this group as rowdy fifth graders and can immediately see that something has changed. They are more mature now and, as a group, they look good. Now comes the hard part.

Day One – Cuyalí

Last night I was a nervous wreck. After an uninspiring trip to Cuyalí to deliver the invitations to the kids (mostly because the teacher showed little interest), I worried if any of them would show up for our group. What made me think that 11-year olds would get up on a Tuesday morning (they have school in the afternoon) and voluntarily attend our *charlas*?

Nevertheless, I wake up this morning excited to get to Cuyalí to see what happens. We are working in a community building called *El Rancho*, a pitiful structure with a concrete floor covered in dust, few windows, no electricity, and a persistent musty odor. In order to access the "building," we arrive early to meet Santiago whose brother is the caretaker of *El Rancho* and has the key. Yesterday, Santiago's brother was not home when I went to remind him we would be by for the key the next morning. Santiago solved this problem by telling his grandmother to tell his brother to leave the key with her, so we could enter in the morning. What a recipe for disaster! Grandma, a wrinkly woman with no teeth, made no indication that she understood the message, much less would pass it along. But, Santiago was not worried, so what could I do?

After a quick breakfast, we are out the door at 6:30 a.m. to catch the bus to Cuyalí. After being dropped off, we have a pleasant walk down the dirt road to the community. A fresh, crisp breeze blows and gray clouds block the powerful sun that will soon beam down on us and make life a little less pleasant.

We arrive at the house of Santiago's brother, and I'm prepared for the worst. "Hola!" shouts Santiago seconds after spitting out toothpaste into a metal tin. He is standing shirtless on the front porch. He leans over to Grandma who smiles but makes no indication she knows why we are here. Santiago yells something, asks about the key, and disappears. Grandma stares at us. "Here it is," Santiago says triumphantly, handing me a key. I'm relieved. "Just come by whenever you need it," says Grandma. I want to hug her. Things are looking up.

Problem number two: *El Rancho*, from what we have gathered, is only used a couple of times a year for dances. There are no chairs, only a few rickety wooden benches running along both side walls. So we decide to ask the school if we can borrow some plastic chairs that they rarely use. The school obliges, and Cristina and I grab them. It's a good 15-minute walk to *El Rancho*, and we immediately realize we are not going to make it carrying all of the chairs. However, this is Cuyalí where a friend is always a step away. A kind man, whom I apparently met once, stops us and tells us to put the chairs in the back of his truck. Problem solved.

It's now 8 o'clock and four kids have shown up: one girl, Irma, a delightful and very intelligent child, and three of the most disruptive boys in the class who are currently riding their bikes in circles in the large open dirt field in front of *El Rancho*. Then two more girls arrive, and we now have six. A success? I don't feel that way, but at least someone has shown up.

Then it happens. One by one, from all directions, they start emerging. I can hardly contain my excitement as more and more walk in the door and take a seat. By 8:15, 20 kids have shown up. Henry, who is notoriously late, arrives at 8:40. Twenty-one of the 26 children have come. For an hour they work hard and more efficiently than at any point last year. Most importantly, they seem to be enjoying every moment of it.

The first activity is from *Odyssey of the Mind*, an international education program that provides creative problem-solving opportunities for students. It is a structured activity in which they work in teams to construct a tall structure. It is an activity that requires creativity and planning, the type of thinking they rarely do in school. For 15 minutes they develop strategies, argue their ideas, tape, and build. All but one of the five teams fail to build a structure that can stand up. This is exactly what we expected, but the kids are not discouraged. This whole thing, the group and its activities, is an experiment. We are trying to create something that will be strong and durable. We are trying to develop minds, teach teamwork, and build self-confidence, and we are trying to do it in poverty. We are trying to form leaders. As long as we are not afraid of setbacks and maintain our faith in the kids, this may just work. It is only day one, and I suppress my excitement. Let's see what happens next week.

Alejandro

No child was the source of more problems last year than Alejandro. He was the only one who appeared thoroughly bored with all of my charlas, showed little respect for me, and was one of only two kids I had to remove from a *charla*. So, when I heard that only 26 students were in sixth grade in Cuyalí this year, I automatically assumed that Alejandro was one of the children that either failed or simply never returned. However, when I arrived in Cuyalí last month to announce the formation of our leadership group, there he was. When we invited all 26 kids to participate, I was certain that Alejandro would not come. Wrong again. On the first day of our leadership group, only four children were on time; Alejandro was one of them.

A light-skinned boy with freckles, big lazy eyes and a mysterious smile, Alejandro is a puzzle to try to solve. When we gave each kid a manila folder to use for our class, Alejandro returned the following week with his folder in hand, decorated with hearts. He can't sit still, usually looks bored, and bothers whoever is sitting closest to him. He likes to wear a baseball cap and usually pulls it down low over his eyes as he slouches in his chair.

I was sure that after week one he would not come back. When will I learn? We just completed week three, and Alejandro is a regular. A kid who rarely said anything productive last year, he impresses Cristina and me with his thoughts and ideas. His behavior continues to be disruptive, and managing him in a large group can be a headache. But his persistence and our patience seem to be paying off. He seems to have taken a particular liking to Cristina, whom he greets each week with a big "Buenos días, Cristina!" While he doesn't always follow our directions, Alejandro treats us with respect. When Cristina made banana pancakes as a snack this week, Alejandro was by far the most grateful.

So, after realizing that Alejandro wasn't going anywhere and even seemed to be benefiting from our work, we decided to visit his home. After the *charla*, we tell Alejandro we will be by to visit in about 40 minutes as we have plans to visit the family of another student first. "Okay!" he says, and takes off on his bike. We end up spending more time at the first house than expected, and Alejandro must have been getting restless. Out in the field in front of the house we are visiting, I see Alejandro riding his bike around in circles, anxious for us to move on. Is he actually looking forward to our visit?

Alejandro's house, a tiny adobe structure that could easily be mistaken for a storage shed, sits off one of the many winding dirt roads in Cuyalí. It's very small, and I am now hoping that Alejandro is an only child. A young woman is standing at the front door as we approach, and I think that she may be an older sister. "Does Alejandro live here?" I ask. "Yes," she says. "I'm his mother. Come in." We pass through the barbed wire gate, a common feature of homes in Cuyalí used to keep animals from entering the yard and house. We take a seat on a wobbly wooden bench. Alejandro's mother, dressed in a tiny tank top with several large holes, and shorts, sits across from us.

She is immediately joined by her three-year-old son and six-year-old daughter who are curious to meet us. Alejandro is in one of the two tiny rooms studying. The mother is very friendly and talks to us about her situation. Alejandro is the oldest of five children, and I guess she was probably no older than 15 when he was born. His father is out of the picture and offers no support. She is unemployed, and it's obvious this family is barely getting by. The house is the smallest I have ever seen, and I have absolutely no clue how six people live here.

As the mother speaks, the three-year-old, covered in dirt and naked from the waist up, pulls up her mother's tank top and latches onto a breast to feed. The six-year-old, wearing only a filthy pair of blue shorts, stares at Cristina and me as we absorb Alejandro's situation. I look up the road and see a young man on a bicycle riding by. He looks at Alejandro's mom and yells something that sounds like, "Hey beautiful, I will be by tonight for some . . . ." I can't make out the last part, but by the expression on Alejandro's mom's face, it wasn't something she wanted us to hear. She looks embarrassed, stares at the ground and babbles something about the stupidity of the man who just passed. I look at Cristina and can immediately tell that she is thinking the same thing. Alejandro's mother is unemployed and trying to support five children in a town where there is no work available. She may be doing whatever it takes.

We speak with her a little longer and ache at the life this very young woman is facing. She is happy that Alejandro comes to our meetings and laughs at the fact that every Tuesday morning he is determined to be on time. She wants him to go to high school next year but has no idea how she will afford to send him. The cost of the school uniform and supplies are too much.

We wave goodbye as we head down the dirt road, glancing back for one more look at the life of Alejandro. If he is to get out of this situation, if Alejandro is ever to overcome the enormous obstacles in his path, it is now obvious he will have to do it himself. His mother is overwhelmed with five children and no money, the "school" he attends is a disaster, and many boys his age are choosing drugs over education. This is difficult to comprehend. Growing up in a family and a community where I had the love and support of so many people, I can't imagine Alejandro's life. What keeps him going? In a town where most kids never reach sixth grade, what is motivating Alejandro? How does he do it?

Needless to say, we leave Cuyalí today with an enormous respect for this young boy who keeps us on our toes. Alejandro is a treasure, and we both now realize that we are blessed to have the opportunity to spend time with him. Our little leadership group will not be the difference in his life, but maybe we can keep the fire burning inside him. He has made it this far against all odds. I didn't think he could or would do it. I didn't believe in Alejandro, but that was before I knew his life. He has every excuse to give up, leave school, and turn to the life that many young boys in this community have chosen. But, he hasn't, and I'm determined now to find out why. I have a lot more to learn from Alejandro, and I will spend the rest of the day absorbing what he has just taught me.

A few months later, Alejandro's mom will be in a serious car accident where three people die, and she is the only survivor. She is seriously injured, requiring surgery to repair her right leg. She will limp around for months until she is able to afford the surgery.

April Misery

Cristina is on a roll. For the past two months, she has been getting up early and heading out for a morning run while I sleep in. However, today she is gone for only about five minutes before she returns. She comes in, wrestles me from bed, and tells me to walk outside with her. I get dressed, rub my sleepy eyes and step out into the morning warmth. It's only 6 a.m., but already it is hot. The first thing I notice is what I believe to be fog. Then I see the sun, a perfectly round orange ball. It's a shade I have never seen before. Something is not right.

Months of illegal burning of farmland in and around El Paraíso has finally taken its toll. For the past two months, fires have raged on the mountainsides as farmers burn their fields to prepare for the upcoming rainy season.

This has been going on all over Honduras and in neighboring countries. One result of the practice is what Cristina and I are witnessing today, a thin layer of smoke that has engulfed El Paraíso and will do so for more than a month. In Tegucigalpa, the international airport is shut down for an unprecedented two weeks, stranding travelers and delivering a blow to the Honduran economy. Pilots can't see the runway.

The month of April is quite seriously a miserable experience. Stifling heat, no rain, and the smoke make leaving our house unpleasant. As a result, most people stay in for long periods of time, leaving only when necessary. In the surrounding communities, the water supplies have dried up. As we head into Cuyalí to work with the kids, we see entire families carrying buckets, searching for water from neighboring wells. Some walk a couple of miles to the nearest community in hopes of finding a source. Then they lug the full buckets back to their houses, fill their *pilas*, and hope tomorrow the water will flow from local pumps. According to just about everyone you talk to in El Paraíso, the months of March and April get worse every year. As deforestation continues at an alarming pace and more and more people clear land to build houses, the climate changes. People talk nostalgically of the old El Paraíso where the weather year-round was cool and pleasant. Now April is the month of suffering, waiting desperately for the first rainfall which will come, God willing, sometime in May.

Grab your dress, Cristina. Today we do a rain dance. We are not alone.

Lockout

I arrive at the *Casa de la Cultura* at 8:15 in the morning for an 8 o'clock meeting. By Honduran standards, I'm very early. There is no one else around, but this is normal. Things won't get started until at least 9 o'clock. I like to be early for everything, and it sometimes drives Cristina crazy. If the movie starts at 7 o'clock, I want to be in my seat, ready to go by 6:50. I want my popcorn and soda and time to spare. I know, especially these days, between commercials and trailers, the movie probably won't start until at least 7:20 or later. Cristina knows this but puts up with me anyway.

So, I enjoy the fresh morning air and have a seat on a bench in front of the *Casa de la Cultura*. At 8:30, I am still alone. By 8:40, I figure something is up. Erika, with whom I am supposed to be attending the meeting to do a presentation, would have called me if it were canceled. So, I head to the Health Center to speak with her. When I arrive, Erika is on the phone. She hangs up, says good morning, and tells me she has just found out things have changed, and we will be presenting at 9 o'clock at the high school. It is 8:50. We race to the main road, catch a bus, and arrive at 9:10. As we approach the entrance to the school, we notice the gate is locked. Several students are waiting patiently inside the school while others join us outside as we wait to enter.

After several minutes, it's apparent no one is coming. Everyone is chatting, seemingly un-fazed, but right now Erika and I are supposed to be giving a *charla* on AIDS prevention. We are getting impatient when a teacher from the school approaches the gate and says quite calmly and matter-of-factly, "Excuse me. I'm sorry. The woman who is in charge of locking and unlocking the gate is on strike today, so she is not available to open it. We are currently looking for another copy of the key." With that, she turns and walks away. Everyone else goes back to talking as if this is a totally acceptable excuse. Maybe it is.

I can't help but laugh. I have this vision of the "gatekeeper," several yards away, marching around in a circle, raising and lowering her "I'm on strike" sign. I like this idea. How many times in my life have I wanted to announce my own personal strike; to let everyone know that something has pissed me off. In Fall 2001, when professional baseball players were threatening to strike, I went on strike. For one year I refused to go to any games (one of my favorite things to do in Atlanta). Sadly, no one noticed, and the Braves certainly didn't feel the strain as I usually sat in the $5 upper, upper, barely still-in-the-stadium seats.

As the teacher turns and goes in search of the key, I have some questions: How did the teacher and others get into the school? If I get in, will I be able to get out? If the key is not found, will Erika try to climb the wall? Before any of these questions can be answered, the copy is found, and the gate is opened. I feel good for the "gatekeeper." Her strike is a success. She has created disruption and proven her value. Sure, the President of Honduras and the Minister of Education set the school budget, local officials make policies, and the principal runs the school, but ultimately, it is the person with the key to the front gate who really is in charge.

Hop Around San Juan

We always head up to San Juan a little early. Cristina sets up the classroom for our *charla* while I make my usual rounds to find a couple of our more forgetful boys and then pick up María.

First on my list is Pedro, who missed our first meeting because he was beekeeping. I stand on top of the hill overlooking his house and shout his name. "I'm coming!" he yells. I just hope in the next ten minutes he's not called off to fix a pair of shoes, collect some honey, or head into the mountains to cut wood for the *fogón*. I'll just have to see.

Next, I head to Darwin's house, a bright young boy who never knows what day of the week it is. He loves the outdoors, a wonderful quality for a young boy in a town where too many kids spend the day watching TV (surprisingly, in a place so impoverished, televisions sets are prominent). Before I can say hello, Darwin's mom sees me and begins her weekly tirade. Darwin, again, has forgotten. She is shaking her head as I approach. "Darwin, that boy, he is off somewhere playing," she says. "As soon as he gets home, I'll send him over." She shakes her head again, dries her hands on her apron, and sticks her head out the front door to see if her son is anywhere to be found. I start laughing at this weekly routine.

Now it's time for my last stop, and one of the best moments of my entire week. It's time to get María. I stand in the doorway and say, "Buenas tardes." Soon, María's grandmother appears with a big smile and waves me in. "María will be out in a second," she says, and offers me a seat. A moment later, María emerges from the room, moving very

174

slowly. There is a step down to where I am waiting, and this can present a problem for the 17-year-old girl who has spent most of her life walking on her hands and knees. She judges the drop, swings her first leg down, grabs the side of the door for support, and swings her other leg around. She looks up with a big smile. She is ready to go.

María was born with severely deformed legs. Both of her legs were inverted from the knee down. In the United States, a simple operation at birth would have fixed the problem. However, in Honduras, María's parents were told their newborn daughter would spend her life unable to walk. (In poverty, something like a wheelchair is a novelty. I have seen several adults move around town on their hands and knees, propelling themselves along with incredible arm strength, while their legs drag uselessly behind. It is an unbelievable sight to see.). In addition, María's sight is hindered. When she reads, one eye is on the paper while the other looks off in another direction. Hers has not been an easy childhood.

Five years ago, a group of doctors from the United States came through San Juan. María was one of two children chosen to go to the U.S. to have a special operation that would permit her to walk. Her parents were nervous but agreed to let her go. María spent six months in Illinois where she remembers how beautiful and cold it was. When she returned home, her legs supported by braces, she could walk.

However, walking is still not an easy task. Family members cannot seem to agree on the details. Some say that the doctors in Illinois wanted to keep María longer and do a second operation that would have given her more mobility. However, her parents, already nervous about her being gone so long, told the doctors to send her home. Others claim the doctors said they would return to San Juan within three years to do a second operation.

María cannot bend her knees, so she swings her legs back and forth. The terrain outside her house is rough, so simply walking out the front door is an adventure. I take one arm, her younger cousin takes the other, and we head to class. A walk that would take most 17-year-olds less than a minute, takes us over ten. Half way there, under a brutal sun, we take a break. Sweating and out of breath, María's familiar smile is stretched across her face. Every week she does this walk without a complaint. She never shows the frustration she surely must feel as other kids race by us. She regains her breath, grabs my hand, and we continue.

Participating in this course is a big step for María. She is an intelligent girl who is well-spoken with a witty sense of humor. However, she is very self-conscious, no doubt from years of stares and laughs about her disability, and is uncomfortable in large groups. This year, she is determined to complete our course. She is challenging herself in new ways and teaching Cristina and me, as well as her 15 classmates, what a leader is all about. She is an inspiration to all of us.

María greets Cristina, whom she adores, with a smile and a kiss on the cheek. We are ready to begin our class, and I am filled with pride as I look around the room at this group of brave young people. Suddenly, there is a sound in the doorway, and I look over. Breathing heavily and with wet hair from a quick bath his mom probably insisted he take, the last of our students arrives. Darwin is here.

Locked Out . . . Again

After a successful *charla* on HIV/AIDS prevention with a group of student leaders at the high school, I am back a week later at the request of the kids to follow up. As I reach the high school, I notice that once again kids are waiting to leave and others are waiting to enter. They are bunched up at the door, which is locked. The public workers are still on strike, but surely this same problem from the week before has been handled by the leaders in the high school. I stand rather impatiently at the gate when a student informs me they won't be letting anyone in until recess. "There is no one to open the gate." I see several teachers chatting away. Their arms and legs are functioning, and I imagine they are fully capable of unlocking a door.

Then, déjà vu. The exact same teacher from the previous week approaches the gate and says, "Someone will be here shortly to let you in. We are currently looking for the copy of the key."

This is it. This is my frustration in a nutshell. In a week, no one has even tried to develop a solution to the problem of the striking gatekeeper. It is a simple example of the larger reason El Paraíso is stuck. I take a deep breath and sit quietly on a nearby bench. There is nothing else I can do.

A Piece of the Trunk, Please

The sun is setting in El Paraíso as we walk down the winding path from San Juan. We hop across a narrow stream and pass a small house on the left. In the backyard are several banana trees, and I can see that in Cristina's mind she is up to something.

In the past year, she has been making beautiful cards out of recycled paper, a skill she learned as part of her Peace Corps training. She enjoys the hobby and has gotten quite good at it. One day a friend of ours gave her a part of the trunk of a banana tree to use when making paper. Cristina soaked it in water and mixed it with the recycled paper. The result was a unique color and texture that made for beautiful recycled cards.

So, eyeing the tree in the family's back yard, she asks me, "How much do you think I should pay for a piece of the trunk?" This is a question that two years ago would have sounded absurd. Now I find myself trying to develop a logical answer. I realize this is a fruitless effort, and I tell her I have no clue what the value of a one foot piece of trunk from a dead banana tree is worth in the Honduran market.

We approach the front of the house. There is no door, just an open doorway, and Cristina says "Buenas tardes."

A rather tall man comes through the doorway, accompanied by several very young children. Cristina introduces us and then makes her request. He clarifies what she wants, smiles, grabs his machete, and disappears into the back yard. As soon as dad disappears, a little barefoot girl chases after him, leaving the other youngsters at the door staring at us in that familiar way.

178

We hear some commotion in the backyard, and a minute later the man is back with a beautiful piece of trunk in his hand. Cristina thanks the man and offers him some money. He refuses by shaking his head and smiling. "Have a good afternoon," he says as we depart.

As we head home, I can't help laughing and appreciating the generosity of Hondurans. I play out this scenario in the U.S. There is a knock on my door. I peep out and notice two people I have certainly never seen before standing awkwardly outside. I either walk away, making as little noise as possible, in the hope that they will assume no one is home; or, maybe, I open the door, very hesitantly. What do these people want? I'm on guard. "Excuse me sir, my wife takes old used paper, tears it up, throws it in a blender, and eventually turns it into cards we give to our family. We couldn't help but notice you have a dead shrub in your backyard. Would you mind whacking a piece off with your axe and giving it to us? We'll wait right here. We'll give you $2.00." What would I do? Probably call the police.

Here We Go Again

Every day is an adventure. Some days are great, and other days I feel like everything is working against me. The latter tests my sanity.

Daniela and four other women from the bar are at the Health Center for their weekly blood test. Today they have agreed to bring their money so that we can go as a group to register for classes at a local job-training center. I'm excited because I believe that the courses will be a boost to their self-esteem and a possible opportunity to learn a skill that could one day allow them to leave the profession in which they are currently trapped.

When I arrive, the women are in their normal spot on the side of the Health Center, out of sight. Years of rejection and discrimination have led these women into hiding. They prefer to go unnoticed.

"Kevin!" shouts Daniela as I round the corner. She gives me a big hug, and the smell of beer on her breath nearly knocks me over. It's 8 a.m., and Daniela is drunk. The other women somewhat acknowledge me, but they're sober, so the greeting is tempered. In the next five minutes I deduce that none of the women have brought their money, and they look at me like they're surprised I thought they would. This confuses me, and they all promise they'll remember next week. My attempts to speak rationally with Daniela go nowhere, so I leave for my next destination, head down.

Onward I travel to the high school for a 9 o'clock meeting with a group of ten youth leaders. They are eager to start visiting local elementary schools to talk with kids about AIDS prevention. We were supposed to meet two weeks ago, but Suyapa, the woman in charge of the group, forgot to tell them. So I've been anxiously awaiting this day, as I fear the kids will start losing interest.

I walk into Suyapa's office, and she is enjoying coffee and a piece of cake. "Hi Kevin," she says, covering her mouth. "How can I help you?" I smile and ask her where I will be meeting with the kids. "Today?" she asks, looking shocked. I want to walk out the door and scream. I know where this is leading. She forgot. Two weeks ago, I watched her write it down on her desk calendar. "Oh yes, I remember now." She doesn't apologize, never does, and asks me when I can come back, as if it's no inconvenience. I tell her next week, controlling my anger. "Oh, there are no classes next week, so it will have to be the week after." Fine. I watch her write it on the big calendar again. I explain to her that I fear the kids are losing interest due to our failure to meet with them, and she nods and smiles and sucks down some cake.

I have one more request. "If you don't mind, I'd like to look over the list of students in the group."

"I have it?" she asks, pointing to herself.

!*#*!$! I catch myself. Two weeks ago, I gave her the list. I didn't want to because I knew this would happen. I asked her, practically begged her, to guard it because I didn't have another copy.

Now, she is scrambling around looking for it. It's gone. "Don't worry," she tells me, she'll have the kids ready in two weeks.

Why would I worry? I breathe heavily, walk outside, and remind myself that getting angry won't do any good. Then, I get angry.

The Fair

I dread this week. The *Feria Agampa*, a yearly festival in El Paraíso, is about to begin. Last year the result was an immeasurable increase in the number of drunks and a murder.

At 4 a.m. Friday morning the fun will begin. A pick-up truck, armed with two enormous speakers strapped to the bed, will begin its round. There is nothing like being awakened by mariachi music blaring through a pair of very poor speakers.

The music will be accompanied by a continuous barrage of fireworks. "Not the pretty, colorful ones," Cristina likes to add. In charge of the fireworks is an elderly man who holds a cherry bomb in one hand and a cigarette in the other. He lights the fuse, tosses the firework, and it shoots up into the air followed by a *"Pow! Pow!"* He looks like he's been doing this for 50 years and by the expression on his face he's thoroughly bored by his monotonous yet very important job. The *Feria Agampa* is about to begin, and I'm looking for the proverbial hole in which to crawl.

A Fair Disaster

It's Thursday afternoon, just one day before the festivities are to begin and two days before the parade that officially opens the *Feria Agampa*. Things were going along fine, but now a very serious problem has arisen.

Cristina is in the *Casa de la Cultura* when Carlos arrives and tells her the crippling news. The parade, scheduled to take place Saturday morning, was to be lead by two distinguished cows. According to the latest information, most likely accumulated from a variety of astonished sources, the cows, the leaders of the parade, have been stolen. Carlos, in charge of having the cows ready for Saturday, is panicking. Cristina, respectful of the apparent gravity of the situation, is trying not to laugh. Carlos leaves in a flash and in the neighboring room a phone rings.

Sonya, the librarian, famous for her imitation of a cow, answers the phone. It's Elena, ironically calling to ask about the very cows that are now missing. Sonya, unaware of the breaking news, asks Cristina for some information. As Cristina explains, Sonya covers the phone so that Elena doesn't hear her laughing. She takes a breath and tells Elena what has happened. "It seems Carlos has gone to see if he can find two other cows," she says.

In a town where it is not unusual to see two cows wandering casually down the street as if they are heading to the market to buy grain, I do not understand Carlos' reaction. However, the yearly fair is a much-anticipated event, and maybe the missing cows were very carefully selected. Somewhere in El Paraíso, the police radio is crackling: "Be on the lookout for two large cows, festively dressed and marching in unison somewhere in or around Cuyalí."

The cows are never located. Apparently, the only other animal in town trained to pull a cart is a donkey. The organizers of the parade are forced to make a split decision due to this new information. The parade goes on, but Carlos' cart is demoted to the back of the parade. Somewhere cows are chuckling.

Give Up?

Yesterday was an awful day. It was the fourth of July, and we were missing home. On top of that, we just aren't very busy. We've now been in El Paraíso 15 months. Our leadership groups continue to be a success, but outside of that we are bored. My attempts to work with the schools have been fruitless as have Cristina's attempts with the local government and *Casa de la Cultura*.

As we lay in bed, feeling depressed, Cristina sums it all up. As a tear rolls down her cheek, she says, "Why does it feel like no one here cares?"

This is the biggest challenge, and one that does not go away. The sad reality is that our only success has been with kids. They care, as do some of their parents. The problem remains that those in positions to make a difference seem indifferent. You look around this town and see so many problems that everything seems hopeless. Unfortunately, many in El Paraíso seem to have accepted that things will never change. Whether it's a lack of motivation on their part, or some serene acceptance of reality that I do not grasp, many people here are unwilling to work for progress. Having accomplished so little of what we hoped, we cannot help but wonder if we are wasting our time.

So we begin to discuss plans to go home early. We agreed that whenever we reached the point, whether after one month or 26 months, that we didn't feel useful anymore, we would head home. We talk about leaving in November, five months early, when the kids will start picking coffee beans, and the town will shut down. This is the first time we seriously discuss leaving early.

We eat hot dogs and drink Coca-Cola, and the day slightly improves. At around 6:30, we are playing cards when Cristina says, "We can't leave. We can't go home yet. Everybody here gets beat down and stops trying. We can't!" I know she is right, and we agree not to talk any more about going home early.

Another Cuyalí Miracle

It's Tuesday morning, Cuyalí day. We get off the bus, walk about a half mile, and encounter our first obstacle. The rainy season is upon us, so the creek is alive and rising. Crossing it used to be no problem; that is, until a nasty storm knocked over an enormous tree which, in turn, took out the poorly constructed, yet functioning, pedestrian bridge.

This bridge situation is a source of contention in Cuyalí. According to some people, there was a large sum of money available to the city government to build a new strong bridge for both cars and people. As is the case with too many things in Honduras, the money disappeared, and what was left was used to construct the pitiful structure that nature removed rather easily a few weeks ago.

The result, I believe, says a lot about the situation in Cuyalí. Nearly a month later, people still do not know how to cross the creek. Some cross it farther upstream where it is much narrower. However, it is still a difficult jump. For the elderly and children this is out of the question. Others try to hop along some rocks that are scattered throughout the stream. The rest roll up their pants and wade across or wait for a pick-up truck to carry them. No one has done anything to make crossing the creek easier.

About two weeks after the bridge collapsed, we saw a councilman standing outside his truck parked next to the creek. We approached him and said, "Hi." We were curious about his thoughts on the bridge, but he had more important things on his mind. He had locked his keys in the truck and was waiting for someone to bring the spare key. This is all he talked about. It's no wonder the people have no faith in government.

We were visiting Rosa María a week ago and asked her about the bridge. She told us that she has not left home since it was destroyed because she doesn't want to try to cross the creek. She reiterated the supposed scandal with the last bridge and shakes her head. "Maybe a group from Spain will donate money and build a bridge for us," she says hopefully. "I hear they build bridges."

This demonstrates the lack of faith they have in their own leaders and also reveals the common belief among many of the poor of El Paraíso that their only hope is to wait for someone else to come along and solve the problem for them. Their lives or fates are at the mercy of outside causes. In their own minds, they are unable to do a thing about the current situation.

Fortunately for us, a pickup truck arrives just as we are preparing to do the rock hop. We safely and dryly cross the creek and head to *El Rancho* to do our *charla*. However, the key is nowhere to be found. Santiago and grandma argue about who had it last, and we tell them not to worry, we'll figure things out. I imagine one of our kids knows how to break into the building. At the school, we find out that the chairs we normally use are unavailable. The kids will have to sit on the floor. Not good. The final week of the second part of our course seems destined for failure. As we are walking to *El Rancho*, trying to devise a plan, a voice from the kindergarten school building yells, "Hola Kevin!" Shouting my name is one of the teachers whom I recognize. She asks us what we are doing, and we explain our dilemma. "No problem," she says, "We have an extra room here. You can use it."

My jaw drops. This is a dream come true. The kindergarten room is spacious and has tables and chairs. It is a few blocks from the elementary school and an amazing upgrade from *El Rancho*. I'm excited. I want to give her a hug. She offers us use of the classroom every Tuesday for the remainder of the school year.

We are shocked and overwhelmed by our good fortune. We should not have been. Looking back, I see how Cuyalí has changed us. When the key to *El Rancho* disappeared and the chairs were not available, we didn't get mad, and we didn't panic. Cuyalí, somehow, would take care of us . . . And it did.

Sun Dance

Can this country get a break? The entire town celebrated when, in the middle of May, the rains came. The smoke lifted, the weather cooled, and we were all happy.

It's now July, and the rains won't stop. We've had too much. In some parts of town, farmers have had their crops wiped out. Rivers and creeks have flooded, burying the hope for a productive harvest beneath their muddy waters. The rains keep coming.

Need a Ride?

It is Tuesday morning and time for another trip to Cuyalí. The road is muddy from two months of heavy rain as we splash our way towards the kindergarten to meet our leadership group. Then we see it. I have to blink twice to absorb the scene laid out before me. A full 150 yards from the creek bed, we are stopped in our tracks. At our feet is the creek. The powerful rains in the mountains have caused a raging current, causing the creek to jump its bank. Now, aside from the normal course of the creek, a second current has formed. It runs directly down the main road, before veering left and flowing back into its bed.

We are joined by several people who are contemplating what to do. There are not many options. We can wait for a passing pickup truck to carry us across the rushing yet still fairly shallow water, or we can do what others are preparing to do: take off our shoes and socks, roll up our pant legs, and wade through the creek. Neither is a good choice. A truck may never pass, and the thought of tracking barefoot 150 yards through water contaminated with garbage and animal and human feces is neither appealing nor sanitary. So, we keep our boots on and attempt a rather futile crossing, sticking to the sides and taking advantage of strategically placed rocks when possible. The process is slow-going, and we ultimately appear stuck. I make a valiant and highly unsuccessful leap to dry land. I come up short, spraying muddy water all over my recently washed pants. Cristina, after using her husband as a guinea pig, realizes she can't make the jump. She finds a large rock and tosses it half way between where she and I are standing. It sinks beneath the current. The creek is deeper than we thought. Cristina is stuck.

"Hola!" Approaching Cristina from behind, barefoot and wading through the creek, is the mother of one of the kids in our leadership group. She is about 50 years old, shorter than five feet, and probably weighs around 100 pounds. She is wearing an old, faded green dress and greets us with a big smile. Our friend eyes Cristina and me carefully and looks at the creek. She says nothing, bends over at the waist, taps her lower back, and says, "Vamanos!" ("Let's go!"). Cristina, eyeing the raging, feces-infested water before her, seems to contemplate this bizarre offer. Thankfully, she snaps out of it, and looks at me with an expression of "Is this woman serious?" Our friend is dead serious. She is still bent over, tapping her back, ready to give Cristina a piggy-back ride. I can't stop laughing.

After a couple of minutes, Cristina finds a better way to cross the creek; one that doesn't require a piggy-back ride on a woman twice her age and a bit smaller. We safely make our way to the other side of the creek bed, ending our unusual morning commute. The kids giggle at my mud-stained pants, and we all enjoy a good morning in Cuyalí.

It is the memory of our friend at the creek that will be with me this day and for the rest of my life. The image of her bent at the waist, willing to risk her own health just so Cristina wouldn't get her shoes wet, is unforgettable. Just by being themselves, the people of Cuyalí teach me lessons about life every day; just by doing what they do all the time.

Careful What You Ask For

Traveling back and forth from Cuyalí on the bus is a pain in the butt, so we decide to solicit the Peace Corps for a couple of bikes. They hook us up with a volunteer heading back to the U.S., and we head to Danlí to pick one up. As we walk it towards the bus terminal, we are hoping there will be room on the crowded bus for the bike. I'm a bit concerned since the buses are always packed.

Walking past the bank, we see one of our neighbors, a young man named Juan whose wedding we recently attended. I say, "Hi," and Cristina gets an idea. Our neighbor has a pickup truck, and maybe he is heading back to El Paraíso. He explains that his truck is back at home, and he came to town with a friend. "This is his car," he says, pointing to an old two-door Toyota Land Cruiser which barely seats 5 people and certainly does not have room for a bike. "Oh, okay," we say. "We'll see you back in town." We start walking away, forgetting we are in Honduras, where people will do anything to help you out. "Wait a minute," our neighbor shouts, "I know what we can do. No problem. Ride back with us."

"How will it fit?" I ask, worried about the response I will get.

"No, no problem. It will work," he says failing to reveal his plan. Oh boy. "It's okay," I say, "We can take the bus." He will have none of it. Our neighbor's friend, Ivan, exits the bank and looks a little confused. Then Juan explains that Cristina, the bike, and I will be riding back with them.

Ivan pops the front seat forward, and Cristina and I slide into the back seat. Then, Juan moves the seat forward, and hops in the front seat. He shuts the door, leaving the bike outside. What is he doing? Cristina and I look at one another with confused expressions.

Then, Juan reaches out the window with his right arm and picks up the bike. He balances his right elbow on the door and pulls his left arm over to steady the bike that is hanging out of the car window about a foot off the ground. He looks at his friend and says, "Let's go!"

I can't believe what I'm seeing. The bike is heavy, and it is a 15-mile, 20 minute drive back to El Paraíso. I am feeling guilty and smiling at the same time. This is Honduras. I realize I have to be careful here because people drop what they're doing, sacrifice their own well-being, and do whatever is necessary to help out. I know Juan's arm has to be hurting, but he never shows any sign of discomfort. He and his friend drop us off near our house. As Juan lets the bike down slowly, I can see him grimace a little. That was not easy.

We thank them both profusely, and they seem confused. We needed a favor, and they did what Hondurans do. The next morning, Cristina is outside hanging clothes to dry when Juan's younger sister peeks over the wall, smiling. "Juan's arm was hurting all afternoon," she says laughing. "He's really sore."

Looking for Members

We have just returned from a morning in Cuyalí and are passing through the park when we see Fernando. "Some of your friends are at the school," he tells us. Translation: Other gringos are in town.

Parked in front of María Garay is a bus, and it sounds like a party is going on inside the school. Music is blaring. Cristina wants to take a look, but I do not. I don't want to be put in a bad mood. We enter. A group of blue-clad gringos is setting up a tent, while others are throwing around a football as the music from the sound system blasts. Some kids are seated, watching in wonderment, while others run around, taking advantage of another day of interrupted classes.

Irene, the director of the school, sees us peering in and approaches. "Come in," she says. "No thanks," I say. Cristina asks her what is going on. "I'm not sure," she replies. "This bus pulled up and they asked if they could put on a show for the kids. I think it's a Christian work."

So, basically, she's not quite sure what is going on. I shake my head, and we walk out. For the next 30 minutes, from our kitchen table, we listen to a Honduran from a local church tell the kids that Jesus loves them. Mostly they just play loud music. They've managed to disrupt the entire school day.

At the end of the "presentation," the gringos hand out some books about Christianity. Then my blood boils. "We'd like to invite all of you kids and all of El Paraíso to a service at the ____ ____ Church in the San Jose neighborhood at 6 p.m. Saturday."

This exact scenario seems to play out monthly. There are over 80 "churches" in El Paraíso. In our short time here, at least three new ones have been constructed. There is a bidding war for bodies to fill them. People in El Paraíso don't feel much loyalty to any of these churches, and they are more than willing to switch if the price is right. It seems the church with the nicest toys or most food will see an increase in attendance. Almost all of the churches are Christian, so what's the difference? I'm a Christian. At this point in my time here, no single thing is dividing the people of El Paraíso and the surrounding communities more than Christian churches. As I write, I know of at least four more being built with money from the United States. El Paraíso needs access to clean water, paved roads, better healthcare, technology, educational resources, and other things that will work to better the lives of all people in the community. "How can telling kids that Jesus loves them possibly be a bad thing?" one may ask. In a country where so many kids suffer, the message can be powerful and life-changing. However, this is not evangelizing. All of the kids in the school are already Christian. No, the point of the circus taking place in the school is to increase membership at a church. To me, this cannot be what Jesus had in mind.

Heartbreak Hotel: July 21, 2005

In the U.S.A., the soccer game measures nothing more than a little blip on a big radar. It is 4 o'clock on a Thursday afternoon, and most Americans have no idea it is even taking place. They have no idea that in a country nearby, families are huddling around the television set. At 4 p.m., Honduras shuts down. In New York City, the heart of American capitalism, the underdogs from Honduras are playing the mighty U.S.A. in the semifinals of The Gold Cup.

At 3:50, Cristina and I are running down the hill from San Juan. In every house and shop we pass, we hear the pre-game show blaring from TVs and radios. I'm trying to explain to Cristina exactly why this game means so much to the people of Honduras. Just eight months ago, the Honduran National team failed to qualify for the World Cup. I remember the cold, rainy night, sitting in *Café D'Palo* with Honduran friends, watching the clock run out on the dream. It was depressing. Hondurans deserved better, deserved something to be proud of, to cheer about. On that night, the future of Honduran soccer looked bleak.

Then came the Gold Cup which is a tournament hosted by the U.S. consisting of teams from Central America and the Caribbean. An amazing two weeks of soccer by an inspired Honduran National team has awakened a country. Today, Honduras has a chance to win the mother of all games. The U.S.A. is ranked sixth in the world. It has 300 million people and a well-organized, high-priced training program that costs more to fund than Hondurans can fathom. A country that is reminded daily of its own poverty and the wealth of its giant neighbor has a chance to forget all of this. Today, they can make history.

I run in the front door, switch on the TV to catch the beginning of the game as I change clothes. Then Cristina and I are heading over to Israel's to watch the game.

Period 1: Minute 1

Just one minute into the game, and while I am shoving one leg into a pair of pants, there is a golden opportunity for Honduras. The U.S. defense makes a monumental blunder, one you almost never see. As an American defender tries to clear the ball from his own end, a Honduran player runs in and steals the ball. There is nothing between him and the goal but a frantically charging U.S. goalie. The goal looks huge, the goalie so small. This is too much pressure for the Honduran who rushes his kick and sends a harmless rolling ball into the hands of the sliding goalie. I can feel Honduras let out a collective groan. So close.

Period 1: Minutes 5-9

We walk rapidly to Israel's house. For the sake of history, I just can't watch this game alone. Israel is passionate about Honduran soccer, and I want to watch with him in case something miraculous happens.

Period 1: Minute 14

Israel is on one couch, Cristina and I on the other. "The U.S. will win easily," he says. He doesn't even want to believe there is hope. Honduras won game one of the World Cup Qualifying round 5-3, and they never scored another goal. Israel doesn't want his heart broken again.

Cristina and I settle in, and I still have no idea for which team I'm rooting. It's a weird feeling. I love my country. I miss my country and never like to see them lose in anything. On the other hand, I know how much this game means to people here.

Period 1: Minute 29

A Honduran mid-fielder blocks an attempt by a U.S. defender to clear the ball. He then makes a beautiful pass, splitting two U.S.

defenders and landing on the foot of a sprinting Ivan Guerrero. He transfers the ball to his right foot and sends a blistering shot past a diving U.S. goalie. As the ball nestles into the back corner of the goal, Israel is silent. It's as if the whole country has stopped breathing . . . and then "GOOAAALLLL!" The Honduran announcer breaks the silence, and the country rejoices. Israel hops off the couch and yells and whistles.

I think I'm happy, but I'm not sure. Either way, seeing Israel so excited is fun. Honduras 1, U.S. 0.

Period 1: Minute 34

It appears the Honduras party will be short-lived. A beautiful pass from the corner begins to descend in front of the Honduras goal. A U.S. player leaps and sends a header over the charging Honduran goalie who turns and watches helplessly as the ball heads toward the open net. The ball seems to hover in the air forever before banging off the post and rolling harmlessly away. Israel grabs his head with both hands and lets out a "whoa." It's looking like Honduras' day.

Period 2: Minute 26

We are more than half way through the second half, only 20 minutes to play, and the Honduran announcers are beside themselves. Every time a Honduran player crosses into U.S. territory with the ball, they both go bananas. Passing the ball back and forth, harmlessly, 45 yards away from the U.S. goal, it seems at any moment the Hondurans will score. "Minute 26 and we are still winning 1-0!" they shout, sounding as shocked as everyone else.

Period 2: Minute 36

Only nine minutes left, and the Honduran announcer sounds like he needs medical attention. Suddenly a pair of beautiful passes leaves a U.S. player in front of the goal by himself with only the goalie in his way. He connects on a beautiful header, but the Honduran goalie reacts with an unbelievable diving save. Israel is silent. Odelia, his wife, is clenching her fist. "This is why I don't watch," she says. "I'm nervous for two hours!" Honduras 1, U.S. 0.

Period 2: Minute 38

The Honduran goalie, seemingly possessed by some outer force, throws his right hand up frantically and somehow bats away what looks like a sure U.S. goal. Israel isn't looking.

Period 2: Minute 40

The Honduran announcer is now screaming, his voice cracking: "Only 5 minutes to go, and we are winning 1-0!" he shouts. I'm so nervous, but I'm not sure why. Odelia has a pillow on her lap that she is squeezing tightly. Israel is leaning forward in silence.

Period 2: Minute 41

It should have been cleared. The game should have been over. If he had just kicked it harder. If the U.S. player hadn't stuck out his foot at just the right time. If the ball had rolled six inches right. If the goalie's hands were an inch longer. It happened so quickly, I didn't even realize. Maybe it was because the Honduran announcer said it in such a soft, devastated voice. At minute 41, with 240 seconds left to play, the U.S. has tied the game.

Israel falls back onto the couch and yells, "FOCK!" I don't know if this is a Honduran expression that I've never heard, or a little play on the English expletive. Odelia absorbs the blow like she has been expecting it all day. It's in this moment I realize I'm rooting for Honduras. I'm sad as I watch the Honduran players try to compose themselves as they watch the U.S. players celebrate. It's not fair.

Period 2: Minute 44

Life isn't fair. With literally seconds left in the game, a beautiful centering pass and a flying header combine for a spectacular U.S. goal. The referee blows his whistle to end the game. Honduran players are lying on the ground. Odelia shakes her head. Israel gets up and walks outside to cool off. He bounces back quickly. This is life in Honduras. U.S. 2, Honduras 1.

Strike

It's a soft rain, one that slowly and painfully soaks you to the core. A youngster is standing on the corner, gripping his notebook and staring solemnly at the closed doors to the school. He doesn't move, just keeps staring. Cristina and I walk past him and realize he doesn't know the school is closed. Or maybe he does but is just hoping if he stands here long enough, the doors will open and he will be invited in to learn. Not today. The teachers are on strike, and another day is wasted in the future of Honduras. The child blinks his eyes to bat away the drops of rain running down from his soaked hair. He looks left and then right. Slumping his shoulders, he heads for home, his empty notebook in hand.

Basketball Cuts

Over the past four months I have been trying, unsuccessfully I might add, to teach the game of basketball to a group of energetic and fairly non-athletic fifth- and sixth-grade girls. We can't complete a one-hour practice without at least one self-inflicted injury.

On the first day of practice, and for the first two months, I had 20 kids. This was impossible considering we had only one basketball. Each kid touched the ball for about a minute the entire practice. They had to be bored. Yet every week, the girls kept coming back for practice. The idea for the team started last year with Blanquita, who wanted young girls to participate in a fun, yet well-disciplined activity. This was something new for the girls, and trying to teach them the order and discipline of basketball has been a challenge. However, like any project I've done here with kids, they have responded.

My practices aren't always fun, and we spend a lot of time working on the fundamentals. This isn't a big deal in the U.S. where kids are in leagues and know they are working hard so that they can play well when the season begins. In El Paraíso, there is no league, and if there were, we would be the only team. So, these girls practice hard, follow my instruction, and realize that we may never play a single game.

After three months of practice, attendance was rocky and some girls (about 5 or 6) started coming only when they felt like it. This was hurting the discipline I was trying to instill. So, at the end of June, I announced that in one month I would select only 10-12 players to form the official team. The group would prepare for a possible game against the high school where the coach had approached me about playing.

As I hoped, only 13 of the most dedicated girls came to practice in July. They wanted to make the team. Ironically, they were not the most talented, but the ones with a passion for a new sport. I announced that on July 26 I would make the first cuts. As the day approached, the girls became more and more nervous--none more than Abigail, a fifth grader who stands about four feet tall and weighs maybe 60 pounds. When she is crouched low and trying to dribble the ball, you can barely see her. To make matters worse, the baskets at the school are 11 feet high. Last year I tried to have them lowered to 10 feet, but the workers told me the backboard was so old that trying to lower them would bring everything crashing down. Poor Abigail must use every bit of her tiny frame to shoot. After practicing her shot for about two minutes, she is dead tired.

On the day of cuts, they all have a great practice. They don't know it yet, but all 13 of them have made the team. I decide to have a little fun.

"Well, girls, good work today. Here I have the list of those who have made the team. I will read the names in a moment. If you are on the list, we will practice next Monday at 5 p.m. If not, I'm sorry, you can try again next year. "You mean we can't come back?" one girl asks. "Yes," I say trying not to smile.

This is too much for Abigail, who is 100 percent convinced she is not on the team. She grabs her head with both hands and begins pacing. I start reading the list. One by one they scream with excitement and begin to form a line. When another name is called, all of the girls already chosen cheer as well. Abigail, pacing frantically, does not see any of this taking place. Soon I have read everyone's name but hers. I pause and stare at my list. "That's all," I say. I pause again, check my list, and then say, "Wait there is one more name here I can't read." Abigail is pacing, seemingly unaware that she is the only one not to have been named. The girls run over to me, and I point to the name, "Abi," they yell. "It says Abi!" Abi looks up, smiles, and begins jumping up and down like Rocky when he reaches the top of the steps in Philadelphia. She can't believe it.

The girls huddle together and congratulate themselves for having made the team. They leave, proud of themselves, and these are the moments I cherish. Seeing them so happy makes me grateful to be here, working in this town. Young girls in Honduras don't ever seem to get to be kids. They don't play and really aren't expected to do so. That is boy stuff. Girls help out in the house. They certainly don't play basketball. At least for now, 13 do.

KOBS

It's another Tuesday morning and time to board another overcrowded bus to Cuyalí. Fortunately, today there is an empty seat, and Cristina and I slide joyfully in. I'm staring out the window, watching life in El Paraíso go by when something catches my eye. I blink twice, pinch myself, and look again. I press my face against the glass, propping both hands against the window for support. My jaw drops. I can't speak. I say, "Cristina, look." Cristina can't see anything because my big head is blocking the window, and I've fogged up the glass. However, as we pass, she glances out the window behind me. "Oh my gosh," is her only response to the news that has changed my life.

It's a simple sign with four gloriously colored simple letters: K-O-B-S. That spells KOBS, and KOBS means the best tasting ice cream in Honduras. It means waffle cones and milkshakes and over a dozen flavors of ice cream to choose from.

Oh, the glory of it all; the way the morning sun is glistening off the freshly painted sign. KOBS ice cream has come to our little town. A tear runs slowly down my cheek. Opening day is Friday. I will be there. Two scoops, please.

Again … Again

Another bus of gringos representing another local church arrives at María Garay School and another day of learning is lost in Honduras. Our neighbor, Lourdes, tells us that the director of the school, Irene, is afraid to say "no" to gringos. Lourdes' new word is Gring-Gos, as in go away. I sympathize with the remark at this point. They're making all of us look bad. Lourdes asks me to talk to Irene. I do, explaining that she is doing nothing wrong by asking uninvited groups not to interrupt the school day. After our discussion, she seems relieved. Irene tells me she will not allow any more uninvited "church" groups into her school. Good.

Waiting for T-Shirts

Upon completion of the leadership training course, we had promised each of the children a new T-shirt. With the help of the kids, Cristina and I designed a T-shirt that symbolized the accomplishments of the young leaders. A friend in town took the design to Tegucigalpa and gave them to another friend to be made. We were told the T-shirts would be sent to us by bus in plenty of time to give them to the children. I had no choice but to trust this.

It is two days before we are to present the T-shirts to the kids in San Juan at a party that will be attended by their parents. Everything is ready to go. However the T-shirts have not arrived. I head over to *Cafe d' Palo*, where my friend works, and inform him of this. He gets on the phone and, after a brief conversation, informs me the T-shirts will arrive tomorrow in a box on one of the buses from Tegucigalpa to El Paraíso.

I'm nervous the rest of the day and wake up the next morning fearing the worst. These kids are used to disappointment, so they won't be crushed if they don't get the shirt. However, we made a promise to them, and they are excited.

I check in hourly at the bus station, but I'm informed that nothing resembling our box has arrived. The last bus is to arrive at 9 p.m., and this is now my last hope. At 8:30 I begin to walk to the station. I wait patiently on a bench. With each passing minute, I'm convinced there is no way this box will arrive. I begin preparing my speech to the kids, explaining what happened. Finally, at 9:30, the bus pulls up. A handful of people emerge slowly from the bus, returning from a long day in the capital. A burly bus driver climbs down from his seat, exits, and opens a compartment on the side of the bus. He begins tossing passengers' belongings onto the dirt. I approach, looking for anything resembling a box. Nothing. He shuts the door, and when he turns I ask him if he remembers picking up a box in Tegucigalpa. "Una caja? Si." I almost jump out of my socks. He climbs back on the bus, reaches above a row of seats and pulls down a raggedy, large brown box. He hands it to me. It has nothing on it to indicate the box is for me. I rip it open, peek at the contents inside, and then say, a little too loudly, "This is it!" The bus driver nods, probably wondering what is so exciting about some shirts in a box. I pull one out, hold it up to the lone, flickering light at the bus station, and smile. The shirt looks perfect. I put the box on my shoulder, breathe a sigh of relief, and rush home to give Cristina the good news.

The Big Day - Cuyalí

It has been five months since we started the leadership group, and I can't believe this day has arrived. We have worked hard, and the kids have worked harder to reach this point. It is 7 a.m., and Cristina and I arrive at the location in Cuyalí where we are to meet thirteen of our kids who are ready to teach others about the prevention of HIV/AIDS. I am excited to see how they do.

Recently, Cristina and I were reading about the devastating effects of AIDS in Africa. The numbers are unreal; the statistics are incomprehensible. But what scared me most about AIDS in Africa were the causes for the proliferation of the disease: poverty, infidelity, lack of sexual education, the inequality of women, and the acceptance of infidelity among the male population. I could have been reading about Honduras. Unless something drastic changes soon, this country will continue to be at risk for a serious epidemic. So what our kids are about to do today, I believe, is so very important.

At 7:15, twelve of the thirteen kids have arrived. We soon realize that Mirna is not present because another Mirna (we have 3 Mirnas), the team leader, forgot to inform her of the time change. Cristina leads the kids toward the creek, which will have to be crossed, and down the road to the bus stop. I head for Mirna's house.

Mirna is in her kitchen making tortillas when I arrive. Her mother gives her permission to leave her work behind (no small sacrifice) and go with me. Mirna changes quickly, and we head for the bus stop. We storm barefoot across the river and are about 100 yards from the main road and the bus stop when I see the bus approaching.

We must run. Where we are right now, the bus driver will never see us. At the exact same time, our 12 kids dressed in blue shirts and carrying red folders, spot the bus. Mirna and I are nowhere in sight. They start yelling for us, very excited and worried at the same time. We don't hear them. The next thing I see is a sight that will be with me forever. It is one of those beautiful Honduran moments that are so hard to describe. As Mirna and I turn the last corner of the dirt road, we see Cristina and the others waiting for the bus. Then they see us. I can now hear them screaming as they jump up and down, a parade of blue and red dots bouncing under a brilliant blue morning sky, waving us on. Out of breath and smiling, we arrive in time.

The kids are excited and nervous as we head into El Paraíso. It is no secret, neither to the people who live in town nor to our kids, that not too many kind words are spoken about Cuyalí. Whenever we tell both children and adults that we work in Cuyalí, they respond with strange looks and ignorant statements. For this reason, we wanted this group of leaders from Cuyalí to come to town to give the presentation. Fortunately, Irene has given us permission to do the presentations at María Garay.

After a motivational talk at our house and a snack, the kids are ready. They enter the school like professionals, not the rowdy 11-year-olds that they are normally. They look impressive in their matching shirts, purchased with funds provided by our friends in the U.S. All eyes are focused on them. They handle the attention beautifully.

The three teams split up and give the *charlas* to groups of fifth graders. It's so much fun to watch them, to see how far they have come. They lead activities, speak with confidence, and work together. They exceed our expectations. It turns out that today we were much more nervous than they were.

We all ride the bus triumphantly back to Cuyalí. I am both thrilled and sad as our young leaders hop off the bus and skip down the winding road to their homes. I realize that this moment, right now, is everything I had dreamed about one year ago in the midst of all the struggles. I recognize that this is it: This is the highlight, the climax of everything we've worked toward. It's almost anticlimactic.

Later that evening we sit at our little kitchen table, smiling. I cannot describe the feeling Cristina and I experience. We talk and laugh about when we nearly quit. We remember sitting at this same table dreaming up these leadership groups. And we remember saying that if four kids in Cuyalí gave the AIDS *charla*, we would consider it a success. Today there were 13.

A Tribute to the Kids

Over the next few days, the remaining kids in Cuyalí as well as the kids in San Juan do the same thing. In total, our young leaders talked to almost 250 kids about AIDS prevention. The crowning achievement of this five-month, 16-week odyssey was that the young kids stayed the course, using their free time to learn and improve themselves. Over that time, only four kids who started failed to finish.

Before coming to Honduras I worked as a teacher for four years in the U.S. and spent time before that working with youth in various capacities. More often than I liked, my ventures failed. I have never in my life been a part of something so special, so inspiring, and so uplifting. I have to thank these kids. They are amazing.

Slow Progress

Since the completion of the leadership groups, we have found a few other activities to occupy our time. Today, Cristina and I have several things planned. I want to begin typing up information on our leadership groups to include in a manual for future volunteers, and Cristina plans to work on the computer with Antonio on some city maps. Then, in the afternoon, we have a library committee meeting in Cuyalí. There, we are working with Rosa María and other community volunteers to solicit a non-profit organization that constructs libraries in eligible communities in Honduras.

With expectations high, we accomplish nothing in the morning. The electricity is out and has been for the past 16 hours. No one knows when it will return. The morning is lost.

We eat peanut butter and jelly sandwiches for lunch and head to the bus stop in order to be on time for our meeting in Cuyalí. However, we quickly notice that the taxi stand is empty, and no buses are running. A friend informs us that due to the high price of gas, a result of Hurricane Katrina, the transportation workers throughout Honduras are on strike. They are demanding the president lower prices.

We decide to start walking towards Cuyalí with the hope that someone will give us a ride. We are contemplating giving up when Israel stops beside us in his red pickup. He is on his way to get his daughter from the high school she attends in Danlí. Without bus service, she and her friends will be forced to walk, and he is clearly concerned. He offers to take us to the entrance of Cuyalí.

We hop in. "This is the way Honduras works," says Israel in response to the transportation problem. "The U.S. sneezes and Honduras gets sick." We drive about half a mile when I hear Israel muttering something and pointing up ahead. It appears we won't be getting very far. In front of us, four buses and about ten taxis are blocking the road, which also happens to serve as the only transportation route to Nicaragua. Israel climbs out and spends about five minutes trying to negotiate with the transportation workers. They will not budge. This is happening throughout the country as part of the strike. No one passes.

Israel, demonstrating the self-control I've come to admire in Hondurans, says nothing as he turns the pickup truck around to take us home. There will be no library meeting today, and Israel can only hope his daughter finds a way home. He will go back to his house and wait and worry. We will go home and spend the afternoon bored and annoyed. Progress is slow, painfully slow, and there is often nothing we can do about it.

That's What Friends Are For

For the second time in two years, Cristina and I are fortunate to be back in what has become my favorite place on earth (my travels are limited): Roatán, Honduras. A tiny island off the north coast of Honduras, Roatán is a paradise-like location with sandy beaches, extraordinary coral to explore, friendly people, and fantastic restaurants. It's still relatively unknown, and other than an occasional cruise ship making a stop, the beaches are quiet.

While rest and relaxation are foremost on our minds, Cristina and I also have other reasons for making the trip to Roatán. Meeting us here are my mother-in-law, Susan, and my best friend of 25 years (we met in kindergarten), Pete. Cristina and I arrive at the hotel first and take a few minutes to breathe in the fresh ocean air and relish in the fact that we are back in this beautiful place. The cab pulls up, and Pete jumps out. In the trunk are two suitcases: one with his belongings and one with the contents we have been awaiting. Pete smiles broadly as he hands over the second suitcase, and I pat him on the back to show my appreciation. After getting settled in our rooms, Cristina and I open the suitcase and nearly weep. What a wonderful gift!

As a special education teacher in the states, literacy instruction was and remains a passion of mine. Cristina and I have been shocked, to say the least, by the lack of reading resources available for teachers and students. We wanted to do something to help, and now we could, thanks to the amazing generosity of our friends.

Since arriving here, I have been sending emails to a close group of friends and family. Those emails have been forwarded to others. As a result, Cristina and I have been amazed by the number of people who have responded to the emails with requests to help us out in some way. We didn't want to ask for assistance until we knew exactly what type of help would be best for El Paraíso. Finally, we asked, and they came through.

The suitcase is filled with classic children's books in Spanish. We take out each one until we are surrounded by a giant pile of new, beautiful, ready-to-be read books. For now we will enjoy Roatán, but we are both itching to get back to El Paraíso and share these books with the kids who will certainly enjoy reading them.

Beta and Mitch

The sun has recently set, and the bells from the Catholic church are ringing, reminding people that Friday mass will begin shortly. Cristina and I are reading when there is a knock on our door. It is Lourdes. She enters, and I can see she is nervous. "Do you have plenty of candles and water?" she asks, her eyes darting around the house, checking our preparedness. "It's supposed to hit tomorrow or Sunday."

Lourdes is referring to Hurricane Beta, the latest in a string of deadly hurricanes that have devastated parts of Central America, the Caribbean, and the United States.

We have candles, a working flashlight, and purified water, so I am not worried. Peace Corps has put us on "stand fast," the second level of our emergency system. It means "stay put so we can find you fast." There are several reasons I am less nervous than Lourdes. First, I have the backing of the U.S. government and Peace Corps. I'm confident they'll get us out of here if things take a turn for the worse. Second, we thankfully don't have cable. No CNN Español to convince me that the hurricane is heading for our living room. But the third reason explains the fear in the eyes of Lourdes and the lack of it in mine: I didn't experience Mitch.

No one calls it Hurricane Mitch, only Mitch. To the people of Honduras, the 1998 hurricane that unleashed all of its fury on the people and infrastructure of the country represents much more than a big storm. Mitch was a living, breathing thing that will forever be intertwined with the history and destiny of Honduras. Mitch killed

5,600 people and left thousands more with nothing. It caused an estimated one billion dollars in damage. As usual, the poor suffered the greatest. Honduras has yet to recover.

It is October 2005, almost exactly seven years to the day of Mitch, and this is on Lourdes' mind. "The mountains will protect us," she says trying to calm her nerves. "They always do." People in El Paraíso thank the surrounding hills for the relatively little damage suffered in the small town. Even Mitch couldn't get to them like he wanted.

Saturday morning I turn on the news. The hurricane has changed course. It has hit Nicaragua and its projected path is to the north and through El Paraíso and the surrounding areas sometime on Sunday evening or Monday morning. We should be prepared for a lot of rain, something the rivers and creeks of Honduras do not need. They are full. I do a quick check of the house, strategically placing towels and buckets to manage the numerous leaks. I check the gutters and the drain pipe knowing that, in reality, I have little control over the situation. Now, we wait.

Around town, it is quiet. People are going about their daily routine, but there is an underlying tension. I wait in line at the bank for an hour reading a newspaper. Around the country people are getting ready, buying water and food, preparing for the worst. President Ricardo Maduro has issued a "Red Alert" for El Paraíso and nearby counties. He is very visible, assuring people the country is ready. I'm impressed with his leadership and sense he has done all he can with the limited resources at his disposal. All he can do now is wait.

I visit Omar at the *pulpería*, and the first thing he mentions is Beta. An Evangelical pastor in the U.S. has predicted that a hurricane will devastate Honduras along with several other U.S. cities as punishment for sins. It is atonement time for thousands of Hondurans. Beta is on a mission from God.

Sunday morning brings ominous dark clouds and a strange warmth to the air. Tropical storm (downgraded from a hurricane) Beta is on his way. He is weaker now, but the rain alone could cause a nightmare. President Maduro is on the television with the mayor of Tegucigalpa, Miguel Pastor. "We're ready," he says, and I believe him, whatever "ready" means. I do one final check of the house, candles, and water supply.

Beta never comes. Sometime Sunday, he changed course, tearing through our neighbor to the south and disappearing. I turn on the news Sunday evening. Maduro and Pastor are in the "storm center" where volunteers from various organizations are busy moving around stacks of papers and answering telephones. It looks like a PBS telethon. Maduro and Pastor are beaming, and I can't help but beam with them. Maduro explains that the threat has passed. The rains will come tomorrow but not in the quantity expected. The two men praise the efforts of both local and international workers, and they brag about a country ready this time. We had learned from Mitch, they say, as if it was not nature that turned Beta, but the solitude and preparedness of an entire population. This is a victory for Honduras, proof that we do in some way control our own destiny, even in the face of nature's fury. In a country of people who expect the worst, this is a special moment. I cheer along with them, Maduro and Pastor. Hurricane Beta just couldn't handle us.

The next two days bring lots of rain. Bridges are destroyed, towns are flooded, and 11,000 are left homeless. But in the end, we were lucky. Had Beta kept on course, the amount of rain it would have dumped on an already saturated country would have had far worse consequences. It has been a very long hurricane season, and I, along with millions of others, hope this is the last.

Election Day

Democracy in Honduras is still relatively new, and despite widespread corruption within the government, the people are anxiously awaiting this year's election. The two major political parties in Honduras are the Liberals and the Nationalists. At this point, I have seen little difference between the two, an opinion shared by others, especially supporters of the three much smaller and relatively irrelevant parties. Hondurans are fiercely loyal to their parties. El Paraíso never elects a Nationalist mayor since a majority of the town votes Liberal every time.

The past two months have been a flurry of negative ads, large rallies, and continuous playing of the campaign songs of both candidates. I find myself singing the catchy tunes as I walk around town. The Liberal candidate is Manuel Zelaya or "Mel." Everyone running for office has a nickname. It's mandatory. He is running a safe campaign, counting on the continuous problems of the current Nationalist administration to thrust him into office. He is promising 100,000 new jobs every year, primarily in road construction, tourism, and other development projects. He hasn't exactly explained where the money will come from, but he's a politician, so why bother. It all sounds good on paper. Mel has a nice smile, friendly demeanor and seems sincere. Most Liberals I talk with say he is incompetent, but he's all they have right now. "He's better than the other guy," they say.

The "other guy" is Porfirio Lobo, or "Pepe." He is a fiery man running on the platform "Trabajo y Seguridad" (work and security). His emblem is a clenched fist. Mel, he says, is weak on gang members, believing they should have more rights than their innocent victims. Pepe has thrown so much mud at Mel that I can't keep the accusations straight. According to the newspapers, Pepe's most influential campaign advisor is from the United States and is an expert in negative campaigns. Pepe says he'll find work for everyone and get rid of the gangs.

From what I gather, Pepe and Mel have one thing in common: They have no idea how to do any of this. Sounds like U.S. politics to me!

November 27th has arrived, and it's election day in Honduras. El Paraíso is awash in red and white, the colors of the Liberal party. Mel signs are everywhere. A few recent polls (I have no idea how they conduct a poll in a country where a majority of the population has no phone and lives in rather isolated areas) indicate Pepe is going to win.

Election day goes smoothly. I watch in admiration as truck loads of people flow in from the most distant mountain villages to vote. They put Americans to shame. Hondurans are very patient people. They have to be in order to maintain their sanity. No problems are reported. Everyone, including myself, is looking forward to 5 p.m. when the polls close and the early returns will start coming in.

People are more excited than usual this year because a new computer system is being used that will spit out the results immeasurably quicker than in the past. The Tribunal Supremo Electoral (TSE) is the official vote-counting body, and this is to be their finest moment.

It is 5:15, and I park myself in front of my six-inch television. The TSE headquarters is hopping. Dozens of volunteers sit at their computers, ready to start entering results from all over the country. I've got the popcorn popping and the Coca-Cola on ice.

At 5:18, Televicentro, my channel of choice this evening to watch the election coverage, releases the results of their exit polls. Based on interviews with over 10,000 voters (from a total of about two million), they predict Mel is the winner by five percentage points. Honduras elects its president by popular vote. At 5:30, in the first indication that this is going to be a very strange evening, Televicentro informs Mel by phone that he is going to be the winner. This is absurd to me, that a TV station is outright declaring a winner with 0 percent of the vote counted.

Now the cameras are on Mel, asking him to comment on his impending victory. I'm expecting a typical politician's response like, "Well, the exit poll results are encouraging, but we all need to be patient and wait for the all the votes to be counted." However, without explicitly saying the words, Mel virtually accepts the results of the Televicentro poll. For the next half hour Mel receives questions from the anchor of Televicentro about things he will begin doing in his first days as President . . . and he is answering!

Meanwhile, back at TSE headquarters, the volunteers are still seated at their computers. They look bored, and the media starts hinting that something is not right. The longer it takes TSE to report any data, the bolder Televicentro becomes with the results of their exit polls. Then, as if things couldn't get any weirder, Televicentro contacts Pepe and basically urges him to concede! Pepe, of course, refuses to concede based on a television poll and adds that his staff conducted exit polls that showed much different results. Plus, he states several times that exit polls showed John Kerry the winner in 2006, and we all know what happened there. Televicentro will have none of it, and the egomaniacs at the station actually seem offended that their results are being questioned. Pepe fails to mention that not a single vote has even been counted yet!

It's now 8:00, the popcorn is long gone, and still there is nothing from TSE. I'm getting sick of watching Televicentro bash TSE and the obvious problems that have arisen. TSE is remaining tight-lipped while Televicentro brags about the "service" they are providing Honduras as the only source of information on election results. How long is this night going to last?

The next few hours are much of the same. Outside the house, a crowd of Liberals is growing and a celebration is beginning. At the Liberal party headquarters everyone is laughing and smiling while the

Nationalists appear to be accepting defeat. I'm beginning to think the head of TSE is going to come on at any minute and say, "Well, our system has completely failed, so we've decided to declare Mel the winner based on television station exit polls."

Meanwhile, TSE headquarters looks like the final stages of a boring party. The computers are still on, but many seats are empty, and the volunteers are wandering around looking for something to do. The media are perched outside the room in front of enormous blank screens that are supposed to be providing continuous updates. TSE, determined to say nothing, gives no hint as to what is taking place inside. I have no choice but to listen to the gurus at Televicentro.

It's now around 10:30, and I'm beginning to lose hope. Then, there is an announcement that TSE is about to reveal the results. The media are frantic, and I sit up on the couch. Three members of the international committee overseeing the transparency of the elections, sit down behind a table. The man in the middle is holding a piece of paper. He says he is proud of how the democratic process has played out in Honduras. He praises the voters and everyone else involved in the election. Now is the moment all have been waiting for. The committee member emphasizes that the numbers he is about to read will be the last update of the evening. Things will start back up again at TSE tomorrow morning. It seems a night full of doing nothing has really taken a toll.

I rub my sleepy eyes and draw close to the television. I, along with the rest of Honduras that is still awake, am shocked by the next seven words spoken: "With 11 percent of the votes counted . . . " Eleven percent! Is this a joke? He continues reading and concludes by saying Mel is currently ahead by four points. The committee members thank the media for their patience (which they have lost) and leave the table. There is no explanation for the delay and no reasoning provided for why the new technology system has counted so few votes in six hours. The media are outraged, and I'm, well, just tired. I go to bed.

The next few days are insane. By the end of the day on Monday (election day was Sunday), 23 percent of the vote has been counted. On Tuesday, people are fed up. In El Paraíso, Mel's supporters claim victory based on the Televicentro poll. They hold a large parade. Mel is acting like the president-elect even though Pepe refuses to concede. He is actually defending his decision to wait for the votes to be counted, like it's some kind of burden to the Liberals. Liberals blame TSE and say that because it has failed, the country has no choice but to declare Mel the winner. Nationalists, shockingly, want to wait until there is actually a winner. Of course, if the situation were reversed, I'm sure the Nationalists would be acting just like the Liberals.

Four days after election day, only 53 percent of the votes are in. Mel is winning by a small margin. Pepe isn't budging. Mel, still not the official winner, begins announcing the cabinet positions under his administration. I'm now imagining a worse-case scenario. What if when all the votes are counted, Pepe wins? Finally, on December 8, weeks after election day, Pepe accepts defeat. He has lost by 4.5 percentage points. Experiencing the democratic process in a country where democracy is young has been fascinating. Over half of the voting population made it to the polls. The media's handling of the situation was very scary, but in the end it all worked out. Here's hoping that the next election will go much more smoothly.

Building a Library

For the past week, Cristina and I have been working in the *Casa de La Cultura*, moving around book shelves and preparing to set up a children's section with all of the wonderful books sent by our friends. Now the day has arrived to bring over the books and place them on the shelves. Another friend, whose mother has worked in a library for many years, donated some beautiful posters that we had framed by a local carpenter. We hang them carefully on two walls that will comprise a section for children and young adults. After carefully placing each book, straightening them over and over, wanting them to look just right, we step back and smile at what our friends have created for the people of El Paraíso. It is evening. The library will open tomorrow morning, and we cannot wait to see what happens.

The reaction to the library can only be described as miraculous. Young children, throughout the day, attack the books, reading them with friends or alone, gasping at each new discovery, and running back to their seats to read the next book they've selected. Middle and high school students are equally excited, grabbing books like *Lord of the Rings* and *Harry Potter*.

For Cristina and me, it is a dream come true. It's what we envisioned over a year ago but never knew if we would witness it. We spend most of the day in the library, reading with kids and basking in their excitement.

Danilo's Journey

The following is a fictitious dramatization of a decision many Hondurans face every day. The main character is a compilation of people I have met and read about during my time in Honduras.

Danilo opens his eyes slowly and rubs them lightly. He blinks rapidly, letting his eyes focus slowly on his surroundings. It is 5 a.m., time to get up. But Danilo's body is begging for more sleep. *Not today, I'm afraid. Today I need this body more than ever.* He swings his legs off the mattress and settles them on the floor. He sets his elbows on his knees and rubs his head. *I have no choice.*

Danilo pulls himself up and grabs his hat from a small nail in the wall. He makes little noise, trying not to wake his friend who has taken in him and his family. Then he walks slowly over to the other corner of the room and gazes down at a site that makes him smile and breaks his heart at the same time. There, crowded on a small mattress, are his four children, sleeping peacefully. Danilo doesn't move. He just stares. *I am sorry I have not given you more. Give me time. I will make a better life for you and your mother. You don't understand now, but you will someday.*

Smoke is pouring from the *fogón* when Danilo enters the next room. His wife pulls a hot tortilla from a small metal pan and adds it to the others. She hears Danilo enter and forces a smile. There will be no tears this morning. This decision was made weeks ago when the rains came and never stopped. She could not argue with him. There is no choice. Danilo takes a steaming cup of coffee from his wife and nods.

226

He has no words left; nothing else to say. So, he turns and walks outside.

The first light of a new day is revealing itself over the plush green mountains. *This is my home.* This *is where I belong.* He takes a sip of coffee and looks slowly to his right. *Why?* There, spread before his eyes, is a large field. Once the source of so much hope, it is now a daily reminder of his misfortune. For the better part of one year, Danilo spent ten hours a day preparing the field. He would grow corn and make enough money to feed his family and improve their lives. Then, a hurricane came and took everything. Beyond the field is a plot of land where his house, the house he built, once stood. *It is too hard. I work so hard and never have anything to show for it. I can't even feed my own children. Now, my house is gone as well.*

Every year Danilo is promised help. The government has a plan. The world has a plan to end his poverty. Every year millions of dollars are poured into his country, but Danilo never sees a penny. *Why doesn't God send his wrath down upon the crooks and politicians who steal every day? Why must I suffer while they get richer? Is this justice? No, I cannot count on anyone for anything. I must do this myself. I am not naïve. I know that if I make it, I will struggle. I will live with four or five others in a small apartment. I will work two or three jobs that others look down upon. I will do whatever it takes. I will pay my rent, buy my food, and send every remaining penny back here. My family will survive. God willing, I will make enough to come home soon. I have no choice.*

Danilo finishes his coffee and returns to the house. His wife is packing tortillas and a couple pieces of cheese into a small backpack. She takes the empty mug and hands him the bag. Inside is some food, a change of clothes, and $200 that a family member gave him for the trip. This, and the clothes on his back, is all he will carry with him. Others are luckier. They have the $4,000 - $6,000 dollars necessary to pay a "coyote," a professional who guides people along a safer route to the Promised Land. Danilo's trip will be a dangerous one. When he walks out of the house neither one knows when or even if they will see each other again. As he stares at his wife, the words come back: *I have no choice.*

There is a whistle from the bottom of the hill. Luis. Danilo grabs his backpack and slings it over his shoulder. His children are still sleeping. It is for the best. He walks down the hill and shakes the hand of his friend. "Don't look so worried, Danilo. God will protect us," Luis says with a smile. "The American Dream awaits us." Danilo can't help but smile at the optimism of his friend. *The American Dream. I have no choice.*

It's Raining Books

Still coming down from our recent high as a result of the newly created children's library, I receive an email from a friend that blows me away. Cristina and I are checking email together when the message comes through. After reading it, Cristina wipes away a tear. This friend of mine, a former classmate in graduate school, works for a company that provides intensive instruction to children and adults with language deficits. My friend is the director of one of their learning centers. She has written to inform me that she has shared our experience with some people in the company, and as a result they would like to donate funds to our cause. I have to read the message twice to fully grasp it all. Cristina and I are floored.

Our initial excitement quickly turns to anxiety. It is February, and we leave for home in about two months. We know we will use the money to purchase books and library equipment for either Cuyalí or San Juan. Unfortunately, Cuyalí lacks any available space. In San Juan, construction has just been completed on a new addition to the school. After meeting with the director, she has offered to give us an entire room in the new building to be used for the library! This is amazing news. Currently, the only books available to students in San Juan are at the *Casa de la Cultura* library in town. We hire a carpenter to construct a couple of bookshelves and then board a bus to Tegucigalpa. We spend most of our time in two bookstores, purchasing children's books, young adult books, educational books, and whatever other books we think would be useful for the kids of San Juan. It's an exhausting day.

We hop back on the bus, carrying bags of new books, and head home to El Paraíso.

Over the next two weeks, an empty room is transformed into a library. Our youth leaders in San Juan help us set it up, and they are buzzing with excitement as each new book is placed on the shelf. Cristina and I take a lot of pictures and send them to my friend to share with her coworkers. They have provided an amazing gift to a well-deserving group of young people.

The One

Helmuth pulls a chair up to the small table, takes a seat and sets down his clipboard. He smiles and looks slowly at each of the ten children from San Juan seated around him. Director of the Peace Corps Honduras Health Project, Helmuth is a passionate Honduran with a heart the size of his home country. After several months of reading my reports about these kids, and a few kind words from other Peace Corps Volunteers aware of our project, he has decided to come out and see things for himself. This is the part of the job Helmuth loves. He enjoys leaving the office, traveling the beautiful countryside, and meeting the fellow Hondurans he has dedicated his life to helping. Trapped behind a desk most days, buried under a mountain of U.S. government paperwork, Helmuth rarely has the opportunity to see the fruits of his labor. He knows someone has to be behind that desk, and he does it without complaining. However, his heart is out here in places like San Juan.

After a few seconds, Helmuth looks to me to begin the meeting. I am nervous. For the past two years I have seen this group of kids grow. I have watched their self-confidence and self-esteem blossom, and I now truly believe that this project has had a positive impact on their lives. However, they are young, and I wonder if, in this moment, they will be able to self-reflect and put into words the things I have seen.

For the next 30 minutes Helmuth talks with the kids. Mostly, they share their knowledge about AIDS and talk proudly of the day they stood in front of other youth and shared this information. "We were nervous, but we did it," they say. "That's what leaders do." I'm beaming.

Helmuth pauses a second and then looks into the eyes of Raquel, who has just spoken. The 12-year-old, with long brown hair and a big smile, looks back at Helmuth. Last year, she was a confused young girl, and Cristina and I struggled to figure her out. When we first met Raquel as a fifth grader, she was a model student. Eager to learn and quick to speak up when something wasn't clear, she stood out among her peers. We were impressed. However, being very smart and well-liked by your teachers can make you an easy target among fellow classmates and unpopular with the boys. Raquel decided to change. It happened about six weeks into last year's course. Raquel showed up at school wearing a baseball cap sideways and a brand-new personality. She looked different, talked different, and even became defiant in our meetings. Cristina and I knew that Raquel was confused and going through a difficult time in her life. When it came time to select the kids to form the leadership group in San Juan, we never hesitated. Raquel had potential, and she proved us right throughout this past year.

Now, Helmuth has a question for her. "Are you afraid that someday you will get AIDS?" he asks. It's an important question, because in Honduras, for lack of awareness and knowledge of ways to protect oneself, most people are terrified of it. Raquel doesn't hesitate. "No," she says, and there is no doubt in her voice. She looks around the room at her friends and says, "And neither are any of them." Now, every one of our youth leaders is nodding his or her head in agreement with Raquel, sending a message that AIDS will not get them. Helmuth smiles.

Raquel is not finished. She stares down at the table and begins fidgeting with a pen. Her voice is soft. "When I started this leadership group, I wasn't happy with who I was. When I looked in the mirror every day, I didn't like the person I saw. I was ugly," she says, never looking up. The room is silent as all eyes turn to Raquel. She lifts her head and stares past all of us, out into the picturesque countryside of San Juan. "Now, when I look in the mirror, I see someone beautiful."

Raquel leans back in her chair and places her hands behind her head. A big smile stretches across her face as she looks at Helmuth. The words are soft and confident. "I am beautiful."

The room is silent. I am shocked. I look at my boss who is now looking at me. He knows we are thinking the same thing. Suddenly, every form filled out, every report filed, and every long hour spent behind a desk is worth it. Any doubt I ever had about leaving my life in the U.S. and joining Peace Corps is wiped away. They say if you can help just one person in your life, you have done something special. And, if you know who that one person is, you are truly blessed. I look at Cristina, and we both smile. Raquel is sitting just a few feet away.

Thank you, Honduras

Singer and songwriter Phil Vassar performs a song called "Just Another Day in Paradise." In it he talks about all of the struggles he faces in his daily life. However, at the end of the day, he is exactly where he wants to be. I have thought about that song a lot over the past two years.

I will never forget the day Helmuth told me I was going to live in a small town on the Nicaraguan border called El Paraíso. The fact that El Paraíso means "Paradise" in English seemed to mock me for our first year in this little town. There were no snow-capped mountains, no beautiful beaches. On the contrary, there was a lot of dust, running water only on occasion, electricity that came and went, garbage strewn throughout the streets, dirty buses packed with sweaty people, and a lack of any community leadership. How in the world could this be paradise? Slowly things changed. At some point during our time here, I began to enjoy life in El Paraíso and even to feel at home. So sitting here, I realize the greatest lesson I learned the past two years is this: Paradise is all around me, if I choose to see it. Paradise is made up of the wonderful people and the beautiful experiences that are found in any town anywhere in the world.

Paradise

The day begins like any other. A cool breeze greets me as I step outside to assess the weather. Down the street, Felix and his sisters are playing in the street. Humberto pulls the tarp off of his tiny cart, preparing to spend the day selling chips and gum. Friends and strangers pass by, waving. Doña Romany is on her front step, sweeping the dust away, talking and laughing with a neighbor. I smile and head back inside. Our time here has almost come to an end, but we still have some work to do.

It is a cloudy day as Cristina and I make our way to San Juan, a walk that has been a part of our routine for the past two years. As usual, we have forgotten something. I tell Cristina to continue walking. I will run back to the house and then catch up with her. No one runs in El Paraíso so, needless to say, a gringo racing down the street attracts some curious grins. I grab the forgotten item from the house and head back out to catch Cristina.

I am walking quickly as I turn a corner and see a young child sitting in a doorway. He is naked, covered from head to toe in dirt, and sucking on a filthy hand. He is the face of poverty, one I never get used to seeing. Up ahead, I see the back of a young girl, about eight years old, walking hand-in-hand with her grandmother. The girl is wearing a backpack. It is 9 a.m., and her school day is over. I shake my head, trying to stifle all of the anger and frustration I feel for an educational system in disarray.

A pickup truck races by, kicking up a storm of dust as it passes me and then the girl and grandmother up ahead. I pull the hat off my head and use it to cover my face. I start to cough, cursing the dust, a source of such misery and sickness for so many in this town. The grandmother covers her mouth, burying her head in her shoulder in a fruitless attempt to escape the swirling cloud. She uses her free arm to pull her granddaughter close.

The dust settles, and my mind returns to the moment. Cristina is far ahead, so I decide to run. I pass the girl and grandmother and continue up the road. Then, I hear it. It's a giggle and then another giggle. Still running, I look down. There scurrying beside me, hair bobbing, backpack sliding up and down her tiny back, is the girl. I pump my arms and kick my legs furiously, giving the impression I am straining, using everything I have to keep up with my young challenger.

Her giggles are contagious, and soon we are both laughing hysterically. So here we are, a Honduran and an American, different in so many ways yet not at all. Surrounded by the poverty and heartache of life in a Third World town, we race down the street, oblivious to everything around us but the sound of laughter and the joy of running.

We reach the end of the street and stop. She looks up at me with a big smile, then turns to wait for her grandmother. I continue on my way, heart pounding and soul beaming. Above the plush green mountains, the sun pokes out from behind the clouds and lights up the road ahead of me to San Juan. I pick up my pace and head into the hills. Just another day in Paradise . . .

Epilogue

We did leave Honduras with one incomplete project, and that gnawed at us as we prepared to head home. However, today that project is a source of great pride. Unable to build a library in Cuyalí with our resources, we researched and found an amazing organization that builds libraries in impoverished areas of Honduras and Guatamala. Unfortunately, we weren't aware of the Riecken Foundation until our last few months. With the help of Rosa María, we were able to organize a group of community leaders and submit an application in the hope of being selected as a site for a brand new, fully equipped library. One of the requirements is that the community set aside a piece of property for the library. The site we initially selected ended up being unavailable, and our application was set aside. We left Honduras worried that the community would not actively pursue a new piece of land. Well, Rosa María didn't give up. She and others worked together to secure a piece of property and resubmit the application. Cuyalí was selected, Rosa María became the head librarian, and today a beautiful Riecken library sits in the center of the community.

I remember our last day in El Paraíso, sitting on the bus, holding Cristina in my arms as it pulled away from the station in El Paraíso. As we moved through town, every corner, street, and house held a memory. Cristina's tears didn't flow until the bus passed Cuyalí and the realization hit: It was over. A two-year emotional roller coaster and adventure unlike anything we had ever known or expected, was over. Cristina cried, and I had no words to comfort her. I stared out the window at the passing terrain, wondering if I would ever see this place again.

I'm often asked what it was like to return home after my time in Honduras. People are curious about the adjustment to life in the U.S. after being immersed in a Third World country. For me, the initial transition was easy. Cristina and I had accomplished a lot, and all but one project we had begun had reached completion. We were grateful for our experience and ready to return home to begin the next phase of our lives. We weren't sure what or where that would be, but, like our decision to join the Peace Corps, we were ready to try something different.

The book has taken over seven years to complete. I'm not sure why it took so long. Maybe it's because, as I stated at the beginning, I don't fully appreciate an experience until well after it has passed. Cristina and I live in Virginia now. We have two daughters, a cute house, and I operate my own reading tutoring business. These days, my Spanish is rusty, and the years spent in El Paraíso seem forever ago. I miss it. I miss the simplicity of life, the generosity of the people, the laughter of the children, the beauty of the countryside. I miss eating *baleadas* every night for dinner and loving it. I miss the time spent working with Cristina, our walks together to Cuyalí, the way the town viewed us as a team willing and able to help. I miss the optimism of the people in the face of poverty, their humility in accepting our help, and the way they welcomed, embraced, and trusted two total strangers.

Time accentuates the positive. They were the most difficult two years of my life. Looking back now, they were clearly the most important as well. "Would you do it again?" I'm often asked. Upon returning home, the answer was a clear and resounding, "No." That sounded rather harsh to some people. At the time, it was the truth. As I said, we had accomplished more than we had hoped and were ready for life's next adventure. I'm not one to linger too much in the past. I do something and move on. I was ready to move on. Now, when I'm asked the same question, my answer doesn't come so easily. Maybe I would.

For now, life is busy with other obligations. For the first time in years, Cristina and I live near our families. We have young children to raise, a house that needs work, jobs that require time, and the list goes on. New challenges arise that need to be faced. El Paraíso taught us to look for the good in everyone and every place; it taught us that together we can do anything. These are invaluable lessons to have learned, and they have changed our lives.

Tonight I'm cleaning up after dinner when Cristina tiptoes quietly out of the girls' bedroom. They have gone to sleep early. We sneak out onto our deck for a little quiet time. The sun has set behind the mountains of Southwest Virginia, and we can glimpse their dark outline along the skyline. I hold Cristina's hand, and suddenly those mountains are in Honduras. We are in El Paraíso on a crisp, clear night. Familiar voices can be heard, familiar scents abound. I close my eyes. I miss it.

An optimist isn't necessarily a blithe, slightly sappy whistler in the dark of our time. To be hopeful in bad times is not just foolishly romantic. It is based on the fact that human history is a history not only of cruelty but also of compassion, sacrifice, courage, kindness. What we choose to emphasize in this complex history will determine our lives. If we see only the worst, it destroys our capacity to do something. If we remember those times and places -- and there are so many -- where people behaved magnificently, this gives us the energy to act, and at least the possibility of sending this spinning top of a world in a different direction. And if we do act, in however small a way, we don't have to wait for some grand utopian future. The future is an infinite succession of presents, and to live now as we think human beings should live, in defiance of all that is bad around us, is itself a marvelous victory.

-Howard Zinn
"The Optimism of Uncertainty"

About the Author

Before entering the Peace Corps, Kevin Finch was a special education teacher in Marietta, Georgia. Upon returning to the United States, Kevin taught in several public and private schools. For the past few years, he has operated a private reading tutoring business. Kevin lives in Roanoke, Virginia with his wife, Cristina, and their two daughters. Visit his website, www.paradiseinfrontofme.com, or email him at paradiseinfrontofme@gmail.com.

29492240R00147

Made in the USA
Lexington, KY
01 February 2014